From Idea to Action

Praise for this book

'Mahbooba Waizi's excellent book vividly captures the long and winding road of women's empowerment in Afghanistan, not only through her work with women across the country but also through her own personal journey.'

Dr. Linda Jones, International Gender Equality and Social Inclusion Specialist

'Mahbooba Waizi tells the story of decades of experiences and struggles...I recommend that all women's organizations, as well as political and economic organizations, effectively utilize this work.'

Professor Sayed Massoud, Kabul University, Canada

'[This book] reflects the labour and dedication of a woman who has spent her life pursuing the ideals of the women of this country... She still continues to walk this difficult and winding road, amplifying the voices of Afghan women to the farthest corners of the world. Professor, we hope to see the publication of many more valuable books from you in the future.'

Dr. Nasima Masoud, Member of the Board of Directors of the Afghan Women Business Council, Canada

'This book reflects Ms. Waizi's innovative initiatives in facing her life challenges and her valuable perspectives on women, and I hope it inspires all women.'

Kubra Zzaifi, Member of the Board of Directors, AWBC, Settlement and Trauma Counsellor, Canadian Centre for Victims of Torture (CCVT)

'*From Idea to Action,* showcases a constructive and practical perspective that instils hope in the hearts of people. It also demonstrates how a woman, through hard work and perseverance, has found appropriate solutions to challenges and problems throughout different periods of history, standing alongside the people, especially women. This approach has led to positive changes and effective steps towards sustainability.'

Zarghuna Walizada, Member of the Board of Directors of the (AWBC), Founder and CEO of Tac Taz Group of Companies

From Idea to Action

Mahbooba Waizi

Practical ACTION PUBLISHING

Practical Action Publishing Ltd
25 Albert Street, Rugby,
Warwickshire, CV21 2SD, UK
www.practicalactionpublishing.com

A catalogue record for this book is available from the British Library and
has been requested from the Library of Congress.

ISBN 978-1-78853-466-6 Paperback
ISBN 978-1-78853-467-3 Electronic book

Citation: Waizi, M., (2026) *From Idea to Action*, Rugby, UK: Practical Action
Publishing https://doi.org/10.3362/9781788534673

Since 1974, Practical Action Publishing has published and disseminated
books and information in support of international development work
throughout the world. Practical Action Publishing is a trading name of
Practical Action Publishing Ltd (Company Reg. No. 01159018), the wholly
owned publishing company of Practical Action. Practical Action Publishing
trades only in support of its parent charity objectives and any profits are
covenanted back to Practical Action (Charity Reg. No. 247257, Group VAT
Registration No. 880 9924 76).

Cover design & typeset by Katarzyna Markowska, Practical Action Publishing

The manufacturer's authorised representative in the EU for product safety is
Lightning Source France, 1 Av. Johannes Gutenberg, 78310 Maurepas, France.
compliance@lightningsource.fr

Contents

Acknowledgments

This book has come to fruition thanks to the support and encouragement of my friends and colleagues. Their role and presence throughout the winding path of writing and compiling this work not only served as a source of motivation but also helped me step by step through their invaluable insights, experiences, and unwavering support. I am deeply grateful to everyone who accompanied me, whether directly or with their encouraging messages.

This gratitude is dedicated to all those dear ones whose support illuminated this work and who were with me at every moment, ensuring that the stories and narratives of this book could reach an audience in the best possible way. Without your companionship, this book would never have taken its current shape, and I wholeheartedly thank you all.

I hope this book inspires you just as much as my friends and colleagues motivated and energized me throughout this journey. This work is the result of our shared efforts, and I dedicate it to all of you.

I would also like to express my heartfelt gratitude to all those who have contributed with their selfless cooperation and invaluable support throughout the process of improving, reviewing the content, and publishing this book. Without a doubt, the realization of this scholarly work would not have been possible without the collaborative efforts and constructive feedback of every one of you.

Foremost, I would like to extend my special gratitude to my esteemed mentor, Professor Sayed Masood from Kabul University, one of the most prominent and influential figures of our beloved country, Afghanistan, both nationally and internationally, whose invaluable guidance and insights in various fields, especially in writing and content development paved the way for me. I also sincerely thank my dear friend and colleague, Dr Naseema Masood, who supported and encouraged me tirelessly in the compilation of this book. Without your companionship and support, this work would not have been possible, Similarly, I am also deeply grateful to Dr Linda Jones for her precise and specialized advice in the technical aspects and the book's publishing process, which has made the completion of this work possible. My heartfelt thanks also to Andrea Johnson, Head of Practical Action Publishing, for her meticulous editing and unwavering support throughout every stage, and to Chloe Callan-Foster for her diligent work throughout the process. I am deeply grateful to the entire Practical Action Publishing team for bringing this book to publication.

Furthermore, I would like to extend special appreciation to all the dedicated and hardworking women who have made continuous and invaluable efforts to enhance the status of women and improve their social and professional conditions. Your invaluable contributions have not only strengthened the social and professional standing of women in various fields but have also rightly boosted their self-confidence and individual and collective capabilities. Your courage and compassion in creating positive and lasting change in the lives of Afghan women serve as an enduring example for future generations.

Finally, I wish to express my deepest thanks to all the women who have been an essential part of our lives over the years. Women who, in times of hardship and crisis, have inspired us with their dignity, perseverance, and commitment to building a better future for their children and communities. I am eternally grateful for the opportunity to walk alongside you and benefit from your invaluable experiences. I hope that this work, as a small symbol of my gratitude, will forever honour your place in the hearts and minds of all.

With the utmost respect and profound appreciation,

Mahbooba Waizi

A dedication to women

This book is dedicated to the women who, with their boundless strength, infinite love, and unwavering determination, inspire and uplift the world. These women, present in every corner of the globe, not only shape their own lives with courage and an indomitable spirit, but also empower others to stand resilient against life's challenges. They stand firm against every form of oppression and discrimination, unafraid to take action whenever necessary. It is from them that communities and families are nurtured, and they continue to move forward, shaping a better future for all.

This book is particularly dedicated to those who have fought for their rights, who have resisted every obstacle and limitation imposed upon them. These women have played a crucial role, not only in today's world but throughout history, raising their voices across every field of life – be it politics, economics, art, or culture. This work honours you, for you have always moved forward with courage and confidence, creating a better world for yourself and others.

In today's world, when we speak of brave and capable women, we see that the greatest qualities of humanity – love, sacrifice, and courage – emanate from women. They have always sought equality and progress, and in every sphere they enter, they achieve remarkable successes through hard work and perseverance. Women, with their strength and resilience, not only improve their own lives but also the lives of those around them. This book is dedicated to you, as a tribute to all your efforts that have made the world a brighter and more hopeful place.

Your unwavering commitment to progress and change inspires generations. What you have built has not only had a profound impact on an individual level but has also resonated globally. You are the ones who, through your efforts, have brought about positive change in different societies, paving the way for a fairer and more sustainable world. You have proven that the will and determination of women can transform today's complex and challenging world into a better place. This book is dedicated to you, to acknowledge your vital role in advancing these changes.

This book is also dedicated to the Afghan women who, in the current circumstances, have been deprived of their basic rights, such as education, training, and employment. Despite the many social, political, and economic challenges they face, these women continue to strive, driven by hope and courage, to improve their lives and the lives of others. Especially to those women entrepreneurs, who, despite the difficult circumstances, have created small and medium-sized projects within their homes, providing opportunities for work and independence to other women. This work honours your efforts to create change and improve the status of women in your society. Your voice remains a beacon of progress and equality.

Lastly, this book is especially dedicated to those women who have not lost hope, despite all the challenges and hardships they face. Women who, despite everything, continue to move forward with unwavering determination toward a better future. Even in the darkest of times, they have kept the light of hope alive within themselves, working tirelessly to build a world where justice, equality, and equal opportunities exist for all women and men. Your hope is an inspiration to all those seeking change and progress.

May your courage and dignity continue to illuminate the path for future generations and bring about positive changes on a global scale. This book is a tribute to you, to your efforts and determination, for making the world a better place and for all the work you will continue to do.

Mahbooba Waizi
    February 2025

Preface

Over time, we have witnessed numerous changes in our beloved country, Afghanistan. These transformations, which have always been accompanied by various challenges and opportunities, have shaped the current state of affairs. This book tells the stories of the efforts and resilience of mothers, sisters, and women who, with boundless love and determination, have taken firm steps toward building a bright future, never losing hope in the face of overwhelming adversities.

These stories teach us that every individual has a unique and special experience, and as an example of effort and perseverance in achieving goals, can serve as an inspiration to others. They show that, despite obstacles and challenges, individuals can continue striving and working towards a better and sustainable future.

The title of the book, *From Idea to Action*, reflects a personal transformative intellectual and practical journey in my life. Symbolically, this title illustrates the process of turning ideas and dreams into reality and the book clearly explains how my initial ideas for improving the status of women and empowering them began to take shape in my mind, and then through effort, perseverance, and overcoming challenges and crises, these ideas transformed into tangible actions.

From Idea to Action is a story full of emotions, effort, and transformation; depicting the life of an Afghan woman amid Afghanistan's constant social, cultural, economic, and political changes. This work specifically focuses on one of the most vulnerable layers of society, namely women, by retelling my life in an honest and engaging way, blending personal experiences with the challenges and victories encountered over the years.

In this journey from the past to the present, memories of life are revealed during different periods of history, allowing a glimpse into the layers of history. Every individual, especially women, when writing their own history must do so in a way that our feelings and thoughts are clearly visible so that the story becomes a useful, living and detailed narrative of life.

Such writing urges us to respect ourselves and the history of our country; a commitment not only to ourselves but to the entire community. A commitment to create a living history, full of emotions and profound meanings, that will serve as an insight into resilience for future generations, enabling them to connect proudly with their past as part of history.

Life is like a winding path, one that we face with challenges and tests, and this book has helped me reflect equally on the difficulties and sweet moments of my life. Perhaps the bitter memories have made me stronger and better at facing those challenges, as well as remembering those sweet moments like a light in the darkness, guiding me toward the future. However, this story is not only a testament to one individual's life but a lesson for future generations as well.

If we look more closely at the changes that have occurred in our beloved Afghanistan over the past decades, we can see that, beyond the concerns intertwined with challenges and opportunities, there is a blend of joy and sorrow. The question that arises is how we can protect the ideals that lead to positive changes and hope, and adapt them to different situations, allowing us to build a stable and resilient future while addressing the issues we face.

This book comprehensively covers my life, my professional activities, and the challenges I faced in my career but I hope that with the publication of this book, I have also been able to take even a small step in answering such questions; illuminating women's contribution to economic empowerment, documenting social and economic movements through the history of the formalization of women's trade in Afghanistan, exploring a journey with deep historical roots from idea to action.

Introduction

This book is a rich and diverse compendium that reviews historical transformations, retells narratives and testimonies, and examines the impacts of social and political changes on individual and collective lives in Afghanistan.

It tells the story of the author's life from childhood to adulthood as she recalls her early years filled with creativity and dreams in elementary school, family support, continuing education and the pathway to success. A journey accompanied by endless challenges, interspersed with marriage and the birth of two children from persistent struggles in studying and earning a master's degree to becoming a professor at Kabul University.

This work also delves into the establishment of the first women's business cooperative in Kabul, considered an historic step towards the formalization of women's trade in Afghanistan. The author goes into detail about the process of establishing the cooperative, along with the challenges and opportunities faced along the way. She highlights how this initiative empowered women, playing a significant role in their economic and social independence. In this book, one of the highlights is the story of a group of pioneering women, who alongside the author took impactful steps towards economic empowerment for women. One of the first significant steps was the establishment of Afghanistan's first Women's Business Council, which served as a platform for greater participation of women in the economic field. Later, the next significant step taken in launching the Afghanistan Women's Business Federation, strengthened the business and economic networks of women for the future and played a vital role in advancing their economic goals.

The history of women's trade in Afghanistan has undergone significant transformations over the past few decades. In 1993, the first step was taken with the establishment of the Khorasan

Women's Business Cooperative, marking the beginning of a transformation in women's trade. In 1995, Women's Community Forums were established with the support of the United Nations Human Settlements Programme (UN-Habitat). Following, in 2003, the Afghanistan Women's Business Council was established, and in 2007, the Afghanistan Women's Business Federation was founded - all organizations that supported women. Ultimately, in 2017, the Afghanistan Women's Chamber of Commerce & Industry was established, greatly strengthening the role of women in business and industry. The formulation and crucial role that these organizations have played in the growth and empowerment of women in Afghanistan's commercial sector is fully explored in this book. The essential services such, networks, forums and organizations provided are discussed in detail – as the author concludes that these initiatives were fundamental in offering women an opportunity to play a more active and impactful role in the rebuilding of Afghanistan's society and economy.

A portion of the book focuses on the progress of Afghan women and the various efforts made to improve their economic and social status through diverse and fundamental programs aimed at empowering Afghan women in various fields. Programs such as *Through the Garden Gate*, launched by the Mennonite Economic Development Associates (MEDA), which helped Afghan women benefit from modern agricultural techniques. Additionally, another crucial program, *House to House* business skills training in Kabul and other provinces, which provided Afghan women the opportunity to learn business skills is described in this book. These programs, along with business skills training, enabled women to learn agricultural skills, specialized training in areas such as handicrafts and food processing, helping them to achieve financial independence.

Much of this woman's life journey retold in this book was carried out under critical conditions and unfolded amidst crises and complex historical and political transformations – from the turbulent days of the 7th of Saur Coup to the tense periods of the mujahideen and the rule of the Taliban, with significant threats and dangers at every turn. Such obstacles with courage and perseverance were overcome in the road to achieving her goals. The author also bravely recounts the painful experiences of forced migration, dangerous travels through mountains and forests, and encounters with armed attacks and looting. The looming shadow of imprisonment in the lives of women is also emotionally recounted – a vivid reflection of the struggles many women have to face.

This book is not just the story of one woman's life – it is an invitation to all Afghan women and women worldwide to write their own histories, record their experiences, and learn from one another to build a brighter future. By showing the paths the author has taken to overcome crises, wars, and limitations, it aims to provide hope and motivation for everyone.

Chapter 1
From vulnerability to empowerment

The journey begins

I have experienced days of war, internal conflicts, and forced migration in Afghanistan, and today, I look out from a different place, with a fresh perspective. I am part of a generation that rose from the ruins and crises, a generation that sought hope and a better future amidst explosions and rubble. From the streets of Kabul, where the joyful days of the past remain in my memory, I embarked on a challenging and difficult journey. Forced migration, leaving home and country, and starting a new life in another place all left deep and unforgettable impacts on me and many others.

In the heart of a peaceful, green landscape Mahbooba reflects deeply on her journey – where it began and where it might lead. Writing the book – from idea to action – helps shape the path through her own words.

I spent my childhood and adolescence in my homeland, Afghanistan, in the city of Kabul, where the people were still unfamiliar with wars and internal conflicts. I describe myself as a kind, sociable, and hardworking individual. From childhood, I have been acquainted with moral and religious values and strive to always respect and assist others. I was born into a family with deep roots in the history of Afghanistan. My father, Syed Abdul Haq, was an intellectual who spent his entire life serving the people and his country. He belonged to a distinguished Syed family in Kabul. My lineage traces back to Mir Waiz Kabuli (may Allah have mercy on him), one of the well-known and prominent Syed figures in Kabul. His lineage connects through Mir Abul Qasim, who is buried in the Shohadayee of Saleheen cemetery, and the grandfather of Mir Waiz Kabuli, who is laid to rest in the Guzar Barana area of old city Kabul.

My early childhood was marked by a remarkable period in Karteh Seh, Kabul. This magical place, at the heart of creation and history, offered a time filled with beauty and excitement. My paternal and maternal homes, located next to Pol-e-Surkh in Karteh Seh, showcased their own beauty. Years ago, this area was known as "Qala-e Parancha," a name that carried the pride and glory of the past. This name evoked images of earthen fortresses with magnificent towers and historical masterpieces in our minds.

Our fortress was accompanied by an apple orchard, where the fresh and vibrant smell of the apple trees serves as a daily reminder of childhood memories. Each evening, the warm yellow sunlight filtering through the trees hinted at a world full of secrets. The tall gates and beautiful paintings, along with the thick walls, created a sense of security and stability. My parents, like guardians of this beautiful fortress, appeared to me as symbols of endless support and care.

The education I received during this royal era allowed me to embrace advanced and cultural thoughts, and to act as a valuable member of both my family and community. But as I entered the third decade of my life, the heavy shadows of war and internal crises gradually began to affect society, shaping a generation that had to face great challenges in order to reach a better and brighter future.

This story is rooted in my life experiences; a place where the complexities of social, economic, and cultural challenges had changed the landscape of people's lives. However, unlike many who succumb to these challenges, I chose to see the vulnerabilities around me as opportunities for progress. Instead of viewing these conditions as obstacles to achieving my goals, I turned them into motivational drivers for change and improvement.

Like an adventurous journey, from a simple and challenging life toward a world full of hope and opportunity, the story of my life is testament to a strong will and resolute determination to build a bright future, even when the world around me was plunged into darkness. It shows that when a person discovers their inner strength, they can turn any circumstance into a chance to create a better world. This story reminds us that great changes start with a small step – the step that moves from vulnerability to empowerment.

In many societies, women are more vulnerable due to gender discrimination, domestic violence, limited access to education and employment, and social pressures. It should be noted that improving the status of women, especially in educational, economic, and social spheres, can lead to the overall growth and advancement of society and establish social justice.

I too have been part of vulnerable social groups, but I was able to move from this vulnerability toward empowerment. Through effort and deep thinking, I made the best use of available opportunities and, by creating new ideas, I worked to improve the lives of myself and those around me, especially women. I don't see my vulnerability as a weakness but as an opportunity for creating meaningful change, and I have managed to uplift both my life and the lives of others.

In facing challenges and seizing opportunities, I have a hopeful message for those seeking identity and meaning in life. I show them that if they have faith in their inner strength, they can build the best version of themselves from the heart of their problems and change the world around them. This is the message I have for those who may feel defeated by challenges: vulnerability is part of the journey of life, but it is not the end. If you believe in your inner strength and recognize it, you can turn any challenge into an opportunity and move from hardship to empowerment.

My message is simple: cultivate belief within yourself, move from vulnerability to empowerment, and change the world around you. I moved from forced migration and internal crises toward a new life, and you too can step from the depths of difficulties toward a bright future.

Educating girls

I was born in 1335 (1956) during the reign of King Mohammad Zahir Shah in Karteh Seh, Kabul, a period many considered the golden age of Afghanistan's history. I completed my high school education in the final years of this era and developed a keen interest in the world of knowledge and culture.

My father, a devout Muslim and civil servant, worked as an inspection manager in the Ministry of Justice. He was a wise and hardworking individual, traits that I have inherited from him. Despite lacking formal education, my mother was deeply committed to ensuring her children received a good education. My eight siblings and I were able to complete our education. I completed my elementary school at Mirmun Khajo School and then attended Shahdokht Maryam High School for my middle school years, which was later renamed Inqilab High School. In 1973, I successfully finished my secondary education at Zarghuna High School and received my graduation diploma.

Looking back on past school years is always filled with sweet and pleasant emotions, as if we are walking through those days with our friends once again. Naheed Knights and I graduated in 1973; a time when, despite our different personalities, we were like members of a close-knit family. Each student in our class shone with their own interests and talents, creating a beautiful catalogue of memories.

Naheed Knights, a kind and intelligent girl, was always top of the class with her exceptional talent in science and mathematics. Along with her remarkable intelligence, her charming smile always attracted everyone. Shahla, with her beauty and grace, won the title of *Miss of the Year*. Gulalai, a skilled football player, had a passion for sports and was always the best on the field.

The schools I attended were known for their organized and disciplined education. Before entering classes, we would stand in orderly lines, and the teachers would treat us kindly. The discipline monitors ensured that students were dressed appropriately. Upon the teacher's arrival, the class captain would greet them by saying "Walal Seet," inviting us to sit down after the teacher acknowledged the greeting. These experiences reflected the strict order and discipline of the Afghanistan educational system.

From beginning elementary school, I was passionate about all subjects and worked hard each year to succeed in every class. One of the classes I attended was the fifth grade, where sewing was also part of our curriculum. The teachers encouraged us with great enthusiasm in this subject. I developed a deep love for sewing and stitching. I even made a child's bedding set, which was chosen for an exhibition at the annual celebration of Afghanistan's Independence Day, held at Chaman-e-Hozuree. This was a joyful experience for me, and I made the most of it.

Each of my classmates, from Hamida and Nasrat to Manila, Gulalai, Bahija, Rabia, Fahima, Trina, Aziza, and Mina Shakoor, added their unique touch to our shared memories. Every day after school, Hamida, Nafisa Ishaqzai, and I would walk home together, enjoying a path filled with laughter and delightful conversations. In class, I sat with Hamida and Nafisa, and we were also together during personal events. One unforgettable memory was attending the party for the anniversary commemorating the birth of the late Najiba Kaihan in Karte Parwan, where we were all present.

Years passed, and each of us took different paths in life. Naheed got married and moved to England, and Hamida also got married. Years later, in 2020, I unexpectedly reconnected with Naheed in London. It was as if time stood still for a moment. Her voice on the phone was full of joy, and she told me that the school days and those happy moments were still fresh in her memory. She concluded by saying, "But above all, it was your lively face and beautiful smile that has always stayed in my mind."

On the night of July 17, 1973 (26 Saratan 1352 in the Afghan calendar), when I was still in my final year of school, Afghanistan witnessed a significant political shift. It was during this time that a military coup led by Sardar Mohammad Daud Khan, the former Prime Minister, and cousin and brother-in-law of Afghanistan's last king, His Majesty Mohammad Zahir Shah, ended the centuries-old Afghan monarchy. In its place, the Republic of Afghanistan was declared.

Reflection on tradition and education

Throughout various historical periods, the education of girls in Afghanistan has been influenced by various factors, including government decisions, cultural and social changes, and political conflicts. Additionally, the educational capabilities and facilities in Afghanistan have varied over time, affecting the conditions for both girls' and boys' education. At that time, many efforts were made in Afghanistan to improve the education of both girls and boys, but challenges such as poverty and cultural, social, and political discord still existed, which could limit the education of girls and boys.

In Afghanistan, the style of clothing for many people depends on cultural, ethnic, and regional differences. Additionally, there are important considerations regarding clothing in Afghanistan that need to be observed, even in academic environments such as Kabul University and other institutions. Men's and women's clothing varied between different regions of Afghanistan. In some areas, traditional local attire is given special attention.

In many regions of Afghanistan, men usually wear traditional shirts and trousers, while women wear pleated dresses and various types of trousers along with a chador/scarf to cover their heads and bodies. In schools, cities, and villages, girls were required to wear chadors and trousers, and there were no restrictions against this practice. Typically, the dresses were black, and the socks were black and thick, not thin. In the 1960s and 70s, especially in the early 60s, it was observed that individuals considered intellectuals in formal settings often wore Western-style clothing and typically did not wear chadors or traditional garments. Many other individuals in personal and informal settings were influenced by Western-style clothing too. This clothing included trousers, socks, short shirts, and even miniskirts. People tried to dress in a way that matched their social group and avoid environmental influences.

Nevertheless, respect for cultural and religious differences remained important, and local customs and regulations needed to be followed. However, there were no official or mandatory directives regarding the type of clothing people should wear, whether Afghan traditional attire or Western-style clothing, in government offices and academic environments.

Growing a family

At the end of 1973 I married someone to whom I had been engaged a year earlier, with the full approval and consent of our respective families. This bond was a turning point in my life, from the moment we began a new life together as a family. Our life followed the customs and traditions of the time, and since then, family values and customs have played a major role for us in shaping relationships and interactions with others. These customs and traditions are sometimes subjective and dependent upon the different influences and experiences from within our combined extended families, all of which have had a significant impact on the formation of our life together. The important point is that every step we take must be based on principles and beliefs that not only help our personal growth and progress but also strengthen our family and social relationships, providing positive effects to future generations.

After starting my family in 1973, I was unable to pursue higher education for seven years due to the need to focus on family responsibilities. I now have two children, and my son earned his degree in law from Balkh University in Afghanistan and a second bachelor's degree in management and administration from the University of London. He is married and has three children. My daughter, after completing her second year at Kabul University in history and philosophy, sadly could not continue her education in Afghanistan due to civil wars and migration. Happily, she now lives in Sweden, has four children, and has studied as a medical assistant, working at a healthcare centre.

My engineer husband was a progressive and respected figure in various social spheres of Afghanistan. He completed his studies in aircraft engineering in Almaty, Kazakhstan, in 1971. He also worked for the development and progress of women in the country. He held great respect for the role of women and mothers, deeply respected women's rights, and supported gender equality within the family. Because of this, despite certain social traditions, he always supported me in continuing my education, pursuing a career, and raising our children. Through personal perseverance and family support, I was able to overcome challenges and achieve significant accomplishments during many difficult times of life.

Our married life started with seven years living in the same household as my in-laws. This experience introduced us to the positive and hopeful aspects of traditional community life. It also gave me the opportunity to express my talents and participate in social matters. My life was different from the blindly followed structures of a traditional society; instead of seeing things in a negative light, I embraced a positive outlook. This optimistic approach based on principles and beliefs allowed me to develop my skills further in both educational and social environments.

Reflections on social principles and beliefs

Mutual respect: *In any relationship, whether in the family or society, respecting the opinions, feelings, and rights of others is one of the fundamental principles that strengthens communication and prevents issues from arising.*

Honesty and transparency: *Being honest in relationships, both in personal life and social interactions, fosters trust and peace, preventing misunderstandings and problems.*

Teamwork and mutual support: *In family and society, supporting each other and working together to achieve common goals can lead to greater success and strengthen relationships.*

Responsibility: *Taking personal and family responsibilities makes each individual value their role in society and contributes to collective growth.*

Education and continuous learning: *Believing in the importance of education and learning for both the individual and society leads to personal and social progress.*

These principles can be effective in improving the quality of life and social relationships, and their positive impact can be passed down from generation to generation.

I have always been captivated by the appeal of social development programs, especially those that aim to improve the lives of women and empower them economically. Along this path, my dreams and goals, coupled with persistent effort, have continuously driven me toward creating a meaningful life and building a peaceful society. A society where active participation of women in decision-making, especially through economic empowerment programs, is essential and fundamental.

I constantly promised myself that as long as I had breath in me, I would strive for growth and development for women, seeking guidance all the while from my faith. This commitment and faith in the importance of actions leading to social justice and balance have always kept me motivated and hopeful. I firmly believe that on the path to improving society, no one should seek reforms that ignore the needs and rights of half of the population.

Chapter 2
The seeds of empowerment

Inspiring women's empowerment

Before attending Kabul University, in early 1974 at the age of 20, a significant step in my progression was when I proudly joined a multi-disciplinary community centre called "Hurriyat" (Freedom). The main goal of this community centre was to create an innovative experience for Afghanistan, where, for the first time in the country's history, both young men and women engaged in artistic, educational, and sports activities together. These activities were conducted in a manner that respected local traditions, cultural values, and social traditions. This experience not only became a memorable chapter in our history but also served as an effective bridge for communication and exchange of ideas among different members of the community.

The aim of such programs, created by a young, aware, and culturally passionate team, was to encourage social activities. The programs included monthly gatherings for exchanging ideas among the youth, reading informative articles, reciting inspirational poetry and participating in sports like table tennis and basketball. We also celebrated national days with enthusiasm. One of the first events we attended was the anniversary celebration of President Daoud Khan's presidency. The ceremony was, held at an apartment on Seda rat Square located in Shahr-e-Naw, Kabul. The venue which belonged to the Shirdel family was provided free of charge for the Hurriyat community gatherings. The event took place in the large hall on the first floor of the house, and my husband and I attended the event together.

The second significant step in my journey of progress was participating in an English typing course offered through a competitive exam at the "Naswan Waqt" Women's Organization.

This course, held near the Cinema Zainab building in New City, Kabul, was a rigorous program that I completed with dedication, achieving top scores. This training not only elevated my typing skills but also greatly assisted me in my official and personal tasks, continuing to benefit me in all my activities to this day. I am proud to have been one of the students who graduated from this course. It is important to note that the esteemed Kobra Noorzai, the first active and hardworking female minister of the country, headed the institute. May her soul rest in peace, in the knowledge that her efforts and dedication paved a bright path for future generations.

Thirdly, I joined the Democratic Organization of Afghan Women in the year that Dr Anahita Ratebzad, was leading the organization. She had founded the Democratic Organization of Afghan Women in 1966 along with other women such as Suraya Parlika, Kobra Ali, Hamida Shirzai, Momina Basir, Jamila Palwasha, Karima Keshtmand, Deljan Aziz, and Najiba Arash, with the goal of supporting women's rights and raising awareness of social issues. Thousands of women have since joined this organization.

With its dynamic and active structure, this organization created an inspiring women's movement and functioned as a highly energetic network. A congress held every three years served as a representative of the will and aspirations of women. The executive council, along with provincial and urban councils, played a key role in demonstrating the unity and determination of Afghan women.

In addition to its extensive services in economic, cultural, social, and educational fields, the organization was dedicated to empowering women and increasing their awareness. It nurtured women like fertile seeds in the soil of Afghanistan. What made this organization a significant historical movement was that it trained female cadres in various professional fields such as social development, education, economy, trade, politics, and culture. These women became the starting point for widespread change and transformation. The Democratic Organization of Afghan Women, like a green sapling of hope and faith, left a lasting legacy and continues to shine as a guiding light in history, leading Afghan women toward a brighter future. Dr. Anahita Ratebzad passed away in September 2014. May her soul rest in peace.

Today Dr. Shafiqa Razmenda is one of the women who remains active as the head of the Women's Conference in Europe, playing an unparalleled role in advancing women's issues. By actively inviting people to participate in various conferences, she strives to ensure that the voices of women, especially Afghan women, are heard worldwide. These conferences are held to highlight women's activities and achievements in various fields, providing an opportunity for experience exchange and progress.

With her extensive experience and deep knowledge, Shafiqa Razmenda has successfully garnered widespread support from various communities and acts as a bridge connecting women on an international level. She has always worked to address women's challenges and problems, offering practical solutions to improve their conditions. As a result, her efforts have had a significant impact not only in Europe but also globally, contributing to the advancement of gender equality and women's rights.

Shafiqa's efforts in defending women's rights reflect her deep and unwavering commitment to improving the status of women in various societies. Through organizing conferences and seminars, she has been able to build an international network of support for women and contribute to improving their living conditions and activities worldwide.

The movement for change

I vividly remember witnessing one of the most transformative movements in Afghanistan's contemporary history – a movement led by the Democratic Organization of Afghan Women, marking a pivotal point in the struggle for women's rights. I had the honour of being invited on that memorable day, March 8, 1977, when International Women's Day was celebrated for the first time in a completely clandestine yet hopeful and courageous atmosphere.

This gathering took place in a house located in the Karte Seh area of Kabul; a house that, on that day, served not only as a safe haven but also as a bastion for expressing the suppressed aspirations of Afghan women. Behind closed doors, our voices were no longer silent or con-fined. The purpose of this gathering went beyond a simple celebration. Women had come together to raise social awareness and speak of rights that, until then, had only been expressed in whispers and heavy silences. Entering the house was accompanied by an indescribable excitement. Each woman who crossed the threshold wore a determined yet slightly anxious expression, joining the small but brave circle. The fear of this gathering being exposed was evident in their eyes, but the enthusiasm beating in their hearts overcame all doubts. The curtains were carefully drawn, and the silence of the streets outside starkly contrasted with the wave of excitement inside the house.

One by one, speakers rose to talk about the necessity of awareness, education, and women's participation in society. Every word that flowed from their lips was a call for change, a pro-test against inequalities, and a hope for a brighter future. For the first time, women spoke about changing traditional and cultural attitudes, other gender inequalities, and even the right to choose. Some shed tears, some nodded eagerly, and some were so engrossed in the speeches that they didn't blink. That day, the silent walls of the house bore witness to the passion and courage of women who no longer wanted to be mere spectators of their own destiny.

Shortly after, with the April 1978 coup, many of us who had gathered in that house shared a common fate; some remained in the struggle, some were forced to leave the country, and some fell victim to subsequent bitter events. But what never faded was the spark that was ignited in our hearts on that special day – a spark that later turned into an enduring flame, illuminating the path of Afghan women's struggle.

That day, women broke the silence. For the first time, women's voices resonated loudly and forcefully in the heart of Kabul, albeit in secrecy. This gathering was a turning point in the journey toward women's empowerment. For the first time, women came together to openly and honestly discuss their challenges and the changes they aspired to. The atmosphere was filled with hope and a shared belief in the power of unity. Among the inspiring women pre-sent at this historic event, prominent figures such as Dr. Anahita Ratebzad, Jamila Palwasha, Najiba Hotaki, Najiba Arash, Zahira Dadmal, and Shirin Jan Ghorbandi remain vivid in my memory.

That day, in that secret house in Karte Seh, we were not just celebrating a date on the calendar – we were igniting a fire that would burn through the boundaries of silence, inequality, and oppression. We were sowing the seeds of a movement that would empower women to step out of the shadows and claim their rightful place in the world. The voices of these courageous women resonated with a sense of defiance, hope, and a powerful call for change. It was not just an event; it was the beginning of a revolution of thought and action, one that would shape the future of generations to come.

Reflections on community engagement

Promoting a culture of voluntary work and encouraging community engagement in social affairs is crucial for building strong, resilient societies. Volunteering fosters a sense of responsibility, solidarity, and empathy among individuals, encouraging them to contribute positively to their communities. By engaging in volunteer work, people not only support local causes but also gain valuable experiences, develop new skills, and form meaningful connections.

In today's fast-paced world, many individuals may feel disconnected from their communities, but volunteering provides an opportunity to bridge that gap. Encouraging people to participate in social affairs cultivates a spirit of collaboration, helping to address pressing societal issues such as poverty, education, and environmental sustainability. When people come together for a common cause, they create a lasting impact that goes beyond the immediate benefits of their work.

Moreover, community engagement strengthens the social fabric by promoting a sense of belonging and shared responsibility. It helps to create inclusive communities where everyone's voice is heard and valued. Governments, non-governmental organizations, and community leaders must play a key role in raising awareness and providing support to encourage people to get involved. Ultimately, a culture of voluntary work and active community participation creates a more compassionate, united, and sustainable society for future generations.

Chapter 3
Transformative memories of women's work

A respectful yet solitary journey

Despite my responsibilities in raising and nurturing my young children, three years after my marriage in 1976, I was hired at the Ministry of Information and Culture. This was during the presidency of Daud Khan, with Dr. Abdul Rahim Naween as the Minister, and Sayed Makhdoom Raheen as the Deputy Minister of Information and Culture. I began working in the Department of Archaeology. At that time, Professor Zemaryalai Tarzi, who had obtained his Ph.D. in Archaeology from France in 1972, was appointed as the General Director of Archaeology and the Preservation of Historical Monuments.

My first experience of work in 1976 began in a completely male-dominated environment in the Department of Archaeology, located in an old building next to the Kabul Museum in Darulaman. At that time, I was the only female employee in the department. Initially, I started working in the archaeology library, but after a week, I was transferred to the administrative section to gain practical experience in areas such as archiving and managing correspondence. Within a year and a half, I gained invaluable experience in these fields.

One of my fond memories from my time in the Department of Archaeology is when one morning, before heading to the office, I was taking my son to the Sheer Poor Nursery in Shahr-e Naw, which is now used as an emergency hospital. While passing through Cinema Zainab Street, Professor Tarzi, the head of archaeology, happened to be driving by and realised that I had more responsibilities at home compared to the men. As a result, he kindly offered that I could work half days instead of the usual 8am-4pm (with the condition of completing daily tasks of course).

Issues that still surprise me when thinking back include security at the workplace and maintaining a safe environment for women, especially considering I was working in an almost entirely male-dominated environment. As a 21-year-old woman in a workplace with about 70 male employees, both administrative and technical, I carried out my duties with calmness and pride and was always treated with respect and appreciation by my colleagues. During the year and a half, I worked in that environment, I never encountered any negative behaviour or actions that would undermine my dignity.

Also unusual is the fact that at that time, several young graduates from the Faculty of Literature Journalism Department, at Kabul University were appointed as specialists in archaeology. All of these individuals were prominent intellectuals who believed in democracy rooted in Afghan values, and their principles were evident in their behaviour and demeanour. At that time, the Department of Archaeology offered a weekly one-hour Pashto language class for Persian-speaking employees, and I was among the students. Dari and Pashto, the two primary languages of the Afghan people, were designated as official languages. I am not entirely sure of the reasons, but I have never encountered this practice of offering such language classes in other government institutions. Such positive principles only added to my positive experiences in Kabul.

Life in the city of Kabul during my time was like a colourful fairy-tale, full of grace and charm. Kabul, like the stories of "One Thousand and One Nights," breathed with thousands of beautiful tales hidden in its streets. The kind-hearted, friendly Kabuli people, with their open minds, warm smiles, and deliberate words, adorned this city. Kabul's heroes and champions, whose mere names evoked tales of the past and symbols of loyalty and bravery. The mothers of Kabul, who never flinched and endured all hardships, were proud, like the stars of the sky, remained pure, bright, and celestial. The purple fields of Kabul's hills and plains, the enchanting beauty of Kabuli women, the bountiful spreads of food, and the sincere and unpretentious way of life filled the city. You would never hear anyone speak ill of them. In Kabul, grace and blessing resided in the dignified elders, the energetic youth, and the kind-hearted mothers. Kabul, the city of dreams, memories, purity, and kindness, where people recall the sweet stories of celebrations from days gone by.

Learning through diversity

After a year and a half of my assignment at the Department of Archaeology, due to administrative changes in the Ministry of Information and Culture, the department's administrative staff was merged with the head office. I was also transferred to the head office. This new environment, full of diversity, was quite different and included employees and heads of various departments. In each office, at least three to five women were performing their duties, and at least 10% of the women were appointed to managerial or deputy positions. Some of the women who held significant positions included Aisha Amir as the Director of the Centre for Publications Management, Gul Ghati Tarzi as the Ceremonial Manager, Sima Rahimi as the General Director of the Public Library of Kabul, and Rahela Rasikh as the Director *of Zhwandon* Magazine, and other women working at the head office played key roles in advancing the goals of the ministry and also displayed significant leadership skills.

Working hours were from eight in the morning to four in the afternoon. During work hours, everyone was busy with their duties. It was only during lunch breaks or in the hallways, during short rest times, or while waiting for the transport buses responsible for employee transfers, that there was an opportunity to engage in conversation and learn more about each other. Both men and women came to work dressed in formal or casual attire, with most of the clothing influenced by Western styles. Women had the right to choose their workplace attire, and wearing a chador/scarf was optional.

Reflecting on that time, the most important thing that comes to my mind was the absence of any form of linguistic, racial, ethnic, or religious discrimination. Even to this day, I cannot say what race or ethnicity my colleagues belonged to. The rules governing employees were respected, and we were unfamiliar with the concepts of administrative or ethical corruption, which made the events that followed more unsettling.

Reflection on the 7th of Saur Coup

On the morning of the 7th of Saur I was an employee of the Ministry of Information and Culture. On that very day, Thursday, the 7th of Saur 1357 in the Solar Hijri calendar (April 27, 1978), the coup took place. As far as I remember, on that morning , the sun had not yet risen, the birds had not yet begun to sing, and I had woken up for my morning prayers, feeling something unusual. From the early hours of the day, the atmosphere in the city seemed different. According to the law, employees would finish work at 1 PM on Thursdays. Coincidentally, I had taken the day off and decided to go to the Giti Haircutting Salon, near the Hanzala Mosque on the way to the Haji Yaqub Shah-e-Naw Kabul intersection. After that, I planned to go to Karte Seh to visit my parents. I was wearing a khaki-coloured high-neck top, narrow long-heeled shoes, and carrying my handbag, feeling happy about seeing my parents and changing my hairstyle on my way back home, where my children and family awaited me.

When I got off the Karte Seh bus at Pamir Cinema Avenue, I realized I had to catch another bus heading towards Taimani area. As soon as I stepped onto the street, I saw people suddenly running in panic in all directions. There were no buses, and taxis, due to the uncertainty of the situation, they refused to take anyone out of fear. I asked someone, "What on earth is happening?" They replied, "Sister, get to your home any way you can, the situation is bad. They say there's been a coup." Gradually, the sound of tanks could be heard from the city centre.

I was shocked and terrified, and everyone was running, looking for a way to get home. I saw a bus driver, who seemed kind-hearted and compassionate, calling out that anyone heading to Shahr-e Naw should get on. I quickly approached the bus. Men and women rushed towards the vehicle, boarding in a hurry, I was among them, without even asking where exactly in Shahr-e Naw it was heading. I thought, wherever in Shahr-e Naw it is, I will get off and walk the rest of the way.

On the bus, as I quietly listened, I overheard various accounts of the situation. Some said that a coup had taken place, that tanks were heading toward the Arg (the presidential palace). The bus reached Qala-e Fathullah, and from there, as I was close to home, I walked the rest of the way on foot.

Similarly, all family members, wherever they were, managed to get home, and each shared different stories of fear and anxiety. Neighbours had gathered at their doorsteps, exchanging news. We learned that the Parcham and Khalq factions of the People's Democratic Party had united to carry out the coup against the government of Sardar Mohammad Daoud Khan, and that his government had fallen. The television and radio were repeatedly broadcasting patriotic music. We all waited for an official announcement and finally, the first official announcement of the coup's victory, led by the People's Democratic Party of Afghanistan, was broadcast by Radio Afghanistan .

The looming shadow of imprisonment

Following the coup, a period of 'return to normalcy' began. Daily life gradually returned to its previous rhythm – businesses restarted their operations, the streets became crowded again, and people resumed their daily routines. However, beneath this outward appearance of calm, subtle and often overlooked remnants of unrest lingered in both the social and political landscape. While the surface suggested a return to normalcy, the internal and external transformations within society were far from stable.

Soon, internal conflicts within the regime – the People's Democratic Party of Afghanistan, initially between its two main factions, Khalq and Parcham, then later Hafizullah Amin and Nur Mohammad Taraki – resulted in Amin's rise to complete power. This marked a period of further intense conflict, with opponents of the regime leading civil wars across the country, plunging Afghanistan into a time of unsettling insecurity. The new government, through widespread torture, arrests, and the suppression of opposition parties, intensified the continuing hardships.

During Amin's rule, I served at the Ministry of Information and Culture, and at that time, I witnessed the arrest of prominent figures, both men and women, every day. In those times, no one was safe from danger, and even the slightest expression of opposition to the regime could lead to imprisonment. Anti-Amin movements were secretly growing within society, and as someone working in the Ministry of Information and Culture, I experienced many of these developments firsthand.

In the heart of these dark and tense days an event was held in one of the halls of the Ministry of Information and Culture, where prominent figures from the press were present. The crowd, already filled with well-known faces from the media, writers, and journalists, was eagerly awaiting the beginning of a program that promised to be full of excitement and ideas from a gathering of diverse minds.

The atmosphere of the hall was calm yet filled with a subtle hum of activity. Around me were both familiar and unfamiliar faces, each lost in their own world. The sounds of murmuring and brief conversations echoed through the air, and amid this bustle, I sat alone, my eyes fixed on the clock, waiting for the moment when the program would begin. My heart was filled with excitement and curiosity and in that moment, my eyes suddenly fell upon a man. He had been sitting in one of the chairs in the hall, right in the middle, and from where I had been seated, I could clearly see him. He was familiar to me; the editor-in-chief of a government magazine, a man who, due to his prominent position in the media world, was always at the centre of attention. A dignified and composed man, well-known among journalists and media activists.

Amid the discussions and exchanges of ideas, suddenly a person approached him and whispered something in his ear. His expression changed quickly. The words he heard seemed to be more than just a simple message. He rose swiftly from his seat and, without offering an explanation, followed the person. The crowd remained in anticipation – time passed, and the program continued, yet there was no sign of him. Later, we learned that he never returned to his life. Sadly, his wife was left alone with their young daughter without news of her husband's whereabouts. It seemed as though he had disappeared on that dark day – as if the earth had swallowed him up, leaving no trace behind.

This incident was just one example of the painful fate many individuals faced during those harsh and dark times, when they were abruptly torn from their normal lives and cast into grim and unknown destinies. Too many spent time in prisons and torture chambers, and if they survived their brave stories continue to remind us of days when every step, every moment, could have been the end of a life like the man siting in the middle of that hall. Of course, such experiences were not just the reserve of men – the looming shadow of imprisonment and torture hovered over all of our heads.

Khatera's Story

One of my female colleagues, who for the purposes of anonymity we will call Khatera, had been imprisoned on fabricated charges due to her love for reading and exchanging books with her friends. Khatera also worked in one of the departments of the Ministry of Information and Culture in Kabul. She had always loved books and believed that only through reading could one step into a new world. But during Amin's rule, this love for books and reading turned into a nightmare for her.

One day, while Khatera was working in her office, the door suddenly opened, and one of the Ministry employees entered. He said that her boss had called her to his office and wanted to ask her a few questions. Khatera, not knowing what awaited her, nervously got up from her seat and followed the man.

When she entered the room, she noticed that another man, whom she did not recognize, was there. She respectfully greeted them and waited. The boss said, "Please go with this person as they want to ask you a few questions." She asked, "Where should I go?" The boss replied, "To another office nearby." She anxiously asked again, "If I don't return home on time, my family will worry, and I have young children." The boss reassured her, "No, you will return soon.

As she passed through the hallway and descended the stairs, she hoped that one of her colleagues would see her and come to her aid. She also hoped her family would be made aware of her situation. Such hopes were in vain – no one was able to help her.

When they exited the Ministry building, a new car, which she didn't recognize, was waiting outside. The unknown man sat in the front seat, and she was instructed to sit in the back seat. At 3 PM they drove her to a place in the Shashdarak area of Kabul. On arrival she passed through a long corridor and entered a room that seemed to belong to a high-ranking officer. They waited for a while in silence. Then, the door opened, and the office administrator entered. She asked, "Excuse me, brother, where is this?" He coldly and ruthlessly replied, "Kabul." His vague answer only heightened her growing fears. Finally, another man entered and gave instructions for her to go to another room – an interrogation room.

Three men were sitting on a bench, and a single chair was placed in front of them. They gestured for her to sit in the chair, which had obviously been used many times for torturing and tormenting innocent people.

"Do you know why we brought you here?" Khatera replied, "No." They continued, "According to our information, you distribute political and revolutionary books to awaken people against the regime. Tell us who else is involved in these activities." She defensively responded, "I love reading, but I have no intention to harm anyone. If I gave books to my friends, it was solely for social reasons, not political ones. I have no political connections with any party or group." They continued to pressure her, saying, "We have witnesses." Then, the door opened and a fourth person entered, a young girl, who upon seeing Khatera, cursed and said, "Yes, this woman gave me a book." After giving her testimony, she was sent out, and the harsh interrogation continued. They tied metal wires around her fingers, connecting the other end to a device that controlled the electric current. They demanded that she name her colleagues. She replied, "Brother, I don't know anyone involved in this." The man standing over her, ready to turn on the device, snarled, "God forbid I have a sister like you. You are betraying the regime." He then tightened the wires and increased the current, causing her to scream involuntarily. The man covered her mouth with a thick, dirty cloth to stifle her scream. Miraculously, someone entered the room and called the interrogator – the torture ceased and he ordered that she be transferred to a cell as he left.

With each step in that long terrifying hallway, the heavy pressure of fear grew in her heart. In one corner of the cell, there was a desk and two lifeless chairs, and in another corner, a small rug – she knew she was to be left alone amid the loneliness, her future frozen in that cold, dark room.

The guard brought a plate of food and placed it on the floor. She spent the night on the small rug, unable to close her eyes. In that heavy silence, her entire being was filled with sorrow and anxiety. She thought about her family constantly, her worries growing; she didn't know how they were and who would feed her children.

In that dark, lifeless room, Khatera spent the night alone, broken by pain and fear. Every moment felt like a century. Her body was numb from the suffering, and her mind was filled with unanswered questions. The next morning, she struggled to her feet and looked out of the window. But all she saw was more grey, cold walls, offering no hope of life. She whispered to herself, "Are my children still asleep? Will I ever see them again?" These thoughts stabbed at her heart like a dagger; the anxiety never left her for a single moment.

The cold, merciless prison walls were filled with the unceasing cries of other prisoners that assaulted the ears and tore at the heart. Khatera, now aware of the bitter truth of this place, knew that it was not just a place of detention, but a centre for torture and interrogation. Deep inside, a silent cry of pain and hopelessness echoed. "How can I escape this hell?" she repeatedly asked herself, as the psychological and physical pressures mounted from all sides. These inner cries continued to swirl in her heart, unanswered, with no hope of salvation or escape. One of the men, who seemed to be a high-ranking official in Amin's regime, had declared, "If Amin's regime falls, nothing will be left." These words struck her deeply, like a knife in her heart. She knew well that during such times, nothing was predictable, and death could come at any moment.

It might be said that luck was the only thing that saved Khatera from this ordeal – three days after her imprisonment Amin's regime did fall. With the arrival of Soviet forces in the country on 26th December 1979, Hafizullah Amin was killed, and Babrak Karmal, the leader of the Parcham Party, came to power. Khatera, like the other prisoners, was freed from prison after this 26th December 1979 (6 Jadi) pro-Russian coup.

Having endured immense physical and psychological pressure, she returned home with a heart full of pain and memories that would never fade from her mind. She never forgot was not only her own fate, but also the fate of other women who, during this dark and oppressive period, became victims just like her, and whose lives were destroyed by unjust systems of governance.

Following the December coup, in Kabul and some other major cities, the urban population saw a significant increase in the presence of women in social and political spheres, indeed the effect of this caused my own life to take a new direction. Firstly, when I was appointed as a professional member of the team publishing the Balkh magazine at the Ministry and later when I returned to university education.

Yet a bitter truth still lingers – the thousands of silent, untold stories of the pain and suffering of people during that time that never had the chance to be shared. Lives that were destroyed behind prison walls, in the shadow of silence and oppression – innocent voices never heard – buried deep in history but remaining in the hearts of all those who bore witness.

Finally reaching Kabul University

I have vivid memories of the day I arrived at Kabul University. My heart was full of excitement and anticipation. This renowned university was located in the heart of the large city of Kabul, attracting young men and women from all over the country. I was one of them. I had travelled from the other side of the city, from the New City of Kabul in District 10, to attend Kabul University. My family had always encouraged me to pursue my education, and now that I was at this university, I felt that my long-cherished dream was coming true.

From the very first day at the university, I met other young women who had come from various parts of Afghanistan. Each of them had a unique and captivating story. I became friends with Sharifa from Herat. She was an energetic girl with long-term goals. I also got to know Hafizah, who was from Kabul as well.

The friendships we established there supported us in our academic journey. Our stories and experiences at Kabul University were shaped through our studies, new friendships, and various experiences. We were all girls with dreams and hopes for a better future. Our journey to gain knowledge and overcome challenges, while pursuing our dreams, was marked by these experiences. The relationships between girls and boys at Kabul University, like in other educational institutions in Afghanistan, were influenced by local customs, traditions, and respect for them, which helped students maintain a successful and respectful environment.

Kabul University provided an educational environment that was free from prejudice, offering opportunities and professional and academic advancement to all students regardless of gender, ethnicity, or religion. Regarding intimate and unbiased relationships at Kabul University, it should be noted that sincere and non-discriminatory relationships between students and different cultures at the university were highly valued and commended. This indicated that the academic environment at Kabul University largely provided students with opportunities for cultural and social interaction and exchange.

In a non-prejudiced and unbiased environment, students could benefit from each other's cultural diversity and backgrounds and learn from each other's experiences. This helped to strengthen non-prejudiced thinking in society and lead to positive development of interactions between different cultures and individuals. Mutual cooperation and respect between students and professors at universities, including Kabul University, were fundamental to creating a successful and positive educational environment. This close relationship between students and professors contributed to excellence in teaching, training, and research and was fundamental in my own career path.

After graduating from Kabul University, I was appointed as a lecturer in the Department of Russian Language at the Faculty of Languages and Literature due to my high grades and upon the recommendation of the faculty's administration, and the approval of the university's academic council. I held this position from 1986 to 1992, during which time I also taught in non-language faculties such as the Faculty of Law, Fine Arts, Geology, Science, and other non-language departments at Kabul University.

Russian is recognized as an important and influential language culturally and economically in Afghanistan. On one hand, it belongs to the Indo-European language family and is related to our official languages, Dari and Pashto. On the other hand, Russian is considered a scientific and international language. Therefore, teaching this language was essential and vital, as it would facilitate business and cultural interactions.

When the Department of Russian Language was established, the curriculum was designed by Soviet scholars. Almost all the main regulations and fundamental topics were taught by professors and experts from the former Soviet Union, including Uzbekistan, Tajikistan, Azerbaijan, and Russia. Additionally, every year, month-long seminars were held for the Russian language department's instructors to enhance their expertise, allowing them to travel to Moscow and participate at the Pushkin Institute.

Kabul University took pride in its significant and impactful role in serving, advancing, leading, and elevating the Afghan community from the very first day of its establishment until now. It is natural that the adversities of the past four decades have affected Kabul University and slowed its progress. Supporters are committed to providing the opportunity to rebuild the damaged sections of this national and scientific asset. Furthermore, it is expected that Kabul University will continue to encourage positive interactions among students from all backgrounds and contexts to promote a culture of education and collaborative participation. Enhancing understanding and mutual interactions among members of the academic community and promoting attention to cultural and social diversity.

Reflections on collaborative interactions in higher education

Exchange of Information and Experiences: In this environment, students could benefit from the expertise and experiences of professors and delve into various topics. This exchange of information could be effective in developing students' knowledge and skills.

Advancement of Research: Cooperation between students and professors could help create and develop research projects. Students could continue their research under the guidance of professors and address important issues for the community.

Interactive Teaching: The use of interactive teaching methods, such as discussions and study groups, is very common in universities. These methods allow students to achieve deeper learning by using each other's experiences.

Participation in Extracurricular Activities: Students and professors often participate in joint social and cultural activities. These activities can contribute to the development of social skills and address social and cultural issues.

Mutual Respect: Respect for one another is one of the most important elements of cooperation in universities. This respect in student-professor interactions and among peers is crucial and helps foster a positive learning environment.

The power of volunteerism

During my time as a student, I had the privilege of engaging in a deeply rewarding social activity that, as a young individual passionate about community service, I found immensely fulfilling. This experience not only gave me personal satisfaction but also highlighted the power of voluntary work in fostering a sense of belonging and responsibility. Engaging in community service as a volunteer allowed me to directly contribute to the well-being of others, while simultaneously developing valuable skills and gaining new perspectives.

This personal experience reinforces the importance of promoting a culture of voluntary work and encouraging community engagement in social affairs. By providing opportunities for young people to get involved, we can nurture a spirit of empathy, collaboration, and shared responsibility. When individuals are encouraged to participate, it not only benefits the communities they serve but also contributes to their own growth, creating a more compassionate and connected society.

Ultimately, my experience serves as a reminder of how impactful voluntary work can be in shaping individuals and communities alike. It's essential that we continue to create avenues for people to engage, especially young individuals, who can bring fresh energy and new ideas to social causes.

Every week, I dedicated my time to volunteering as a literacy teacher, instructing five women in basic literacy skills. This class was held in the area of Karte Sakhi, close to Kabul University, and it was a venture I initiated with great enthusiasm, driven by a sincere desire to share my knowledge and make a meaningful contribution during my studies.

I accepted the idea that if every educated person teaches one person to read and write, a knowledgeable and enlightened society will ultimately emerge. This belief not only holds importance on an individual level but also has deep and far-reaching impacts on the society at large. However, what strikes me the most is the unparalleled role of mothers. When a mother is educated, her influence extends not only to her children but to the entire family environment and even the community in which she lives. Educated mothers raise generations that understand the value of knowledge and awareness, and in turn, strive to achieve greater aspirations for themselves and their communities.

This cycle of knowledge, passed from mother to child, can bring about significant changes in society. An educated mother builds a bright future for her child, and this path gradually leads to an informed, advanced, and dynamic society. This idea has led me to the belief that a mother's education is the education of society, and investing in the education of women is the key to achieving a sustainable and successful community.

At the same time, once a month, I also had the opportunity to work closely with a professor from Azerbaijan. This collaboration allowed me to teach the girls living in the Kabul University dormitory how to bake cakes and pastries. Using a straightforward approach, we worked together to create delicious treats. This initiative not only honed their culinary skills but also fostered stronger social bonds among the girls. As they learned and worked together, they developed a sense of accomplishment and pride in their ability to produce something of value for themselves and their community.

In addition to these activities, I spent some of my free time at home crafting handmade baby bedding. This bedding, which I had won an award for as the best hand-sewn item during my elementary school years, was donated to friends in need. I received a modest payment in return, but more often than not, I offered the service as a gift, believing that sharing one's skills with others is not only a generous act but also a deeply humane way to make a positive difference.

Throughout these experiences of volunteering, my core aim was always to create a positive impact in society and provide support to those in need. The lessons I learned during this time have stayed with me – even the smallest gestures can improve the lives of others. This realisation became one of the most valuable aspects of my student years, shaping my understanding of the power of volunteerism and the profound effects it can have on individuals and communities alike.

Reflections on useful leisure time

In today's world, where rapid changes and endless opportunities are constantly unfolding, the rational use of leisure time has become one of the most important principles of success. This is especially true for young people, who are at a stage in life where their future is in their hands. Time is considered one of the most valuable resources, and the importance of using it effectively to achieve personal and social goals is undeniable.

Young people naturally face a lot of leisure time, but this time can be used in two ways: one aimlessly and the other purposefully and constructively. The choice between these two can have a profound impact on an individual's future. If time is not managed properly, one may fall into lethargy and lack of motivation, but when used correctly, it can contribute to personal growth, education, learning new skills, and even building meaningful relationships.

The first step in making good use of time is prioritization. Young people must understand which activities are more important in achieving their goals. This can include studying, exercising, learning new skills, or even sharing experiences with others. Moreover, young people can use their leisure time to develop their passions, which could eventually turn into professional careers.

The second important point is finding balance. While using time productively is essential, it should be remembered that rest and relaxation are also necessary. To achieve sustainable success, young people need time to unwind and recharge so that they can continue their activities at their best.

Ultimately, the effective use of leisure time means using time in a way that leads to personal, social, and professional growth. Young people who can make the most of their time not only enjoy their experiences but are also recognized as impactful and successful individuals in society. This ability not only contributes to personal success but also helps in the progress and flourishing of the community. Therefore, young people should always remember that time is one of their greatest assets and the rational use of leisure time is a path to building a bright and successful future.

Chapter 4
A step toward economic empowerment of women

Establishment of the First Women's Cooperative

In the mid-1990s, the establishment of the first women's handicraft sewing and weaving cooperative in Afghanistan marked a significant milestone in the path toward women's empowerment and economic independence in the country. This initiative not only enabled Afghan women to become economically independent, but it also encouraged them to collectively and collaboratively work toward achieving their common goals. In fact, the creation of this cooperative represented a major shift in the history of women's involvement in investment and entrepreneurship in Afghanistan.

The women's sewing and weaving handicraft cooperative in Afghanistan, as the first official institution specifically created for Afghan women, provided them with the opportunity to work together and achieve economic self-sufficiency. This cooperative played a significant role in improving the economic and social status of women by creating job opportunities, offering professional training, and providing financial and social support.

From the very beginning, my like-minded friends and I decided with full determination and motivation to not only help ourselves but also support other women in reaching their goals. This journey, which was considered a novel phenomenon for women at the time, was filled with challenges. However, with self-belief and faith in the power of effort and will, we were able to turn innovative ideas into reality and continue progressing.

The establishment of the first cooperative "Khorasan Sewing and Weaving Cooperative" in Afghanistan, which was officially registered by law fills me with pride.

The cooperative's activities included:

Production: Design and production of various children's, women's, and men's clothing, along with the creation of tablecloths and other household textiles in various sizes and designs, tailored to the tastes and needs of customers. Additionally, housewives contributed to the production of felt, carpets, woven fabrics, and embroidery by hand.

Education: Organizing literacy and English language courses to improve women's basic and social skills and provide educational opportunities for their personal and professional development.

Professional Skills Training: Offering specialized courses in various fields such as sewing, cutting, design, carpet weaving, kilim weaving, crochet weaving, and other handcraft techniques with the goal of empowering women in work and economic sectors.

Training and Awareness: Providing training and awareness on women's rights and responsibilities in society to strengthen their active participation in social and economic matters.

Management: Organizing and overseeing the activities of the General Assembly, Executive Committee, and sections related to finance, administration, marketing, and membership development to ensure the effective functioning and continuous growth of the cooperative.

In a corner of Kabul, in the heart of Afghanistan, which was always grappling with significant challenges, a story began that brought about profound changes. It was a story of women who, in the midst of darkness and hardship, managed to ignite a light of hope for themselves and their families.

At the beginning of this journey, many women either lacked education or struggled to meet the demands of daily life. But one day, a memorable day, an opportunity was given to them. An opportunity that came in the form of a women's cooperative. This cooperative not only sparked the chance to learn various skills but also opened the door for women to enter the labour market and economy.

Widows and impoverished women, who had lived in hardship day and night, shouldering heavy responsibilities, could now begin their production activities using the raw materials provided by this cooperative. This was not just a business, but an opportunity to rebuild shattered lives and improve the economic situation of families. Homes turned into workshops that not only filled the hands of women but also empowered them to become the breadwinners of their families.

The spirit of teamwork was vital on this path. Women learned to collaborate, share their knowledge and skills, and solve problems together. This cooperation not only helped them address their personal challenges but also nurtured their management and leadership skills in the workplace. Their self-confidence grew daily, and they now had the courage to face life's challenges.

However, these changes were only possible through education and skills training. Training courses in business, management, and economics were conducted to help women acquire the necessary skills to advance the cooperative's goals. These courses not only helped them progress in their personal lives but also opened new opportunities for them to have a meaningful presence in various economic and social fields.

This effort was led by me, someone who transitioned from teaching to business. I was teaching at Kabul University at that time and worked at the cooperative every day from noon to evening. This experience was amazing for me. Teaching and business intertwined, with a strong social dimension. Every day, more than a thousand women were directly trained and supported, and their families also benefited from these changes. Indirectly, the effects of this work spread throughout different areas of Kabul, and the community gradually started to transform.

Amidst the many challenges Afghanistan faced, this cooperative provided women with an opportunity they had never imagined before. In a time when many doors were closed to women, this was the only gateway that remained open. Cooperatives, women's businesses, and their presence in economic fields represented a courage that blossomed in the heart of this patriarchal society. This presence was not only important for the women themselves but was also significant for all of Afghanistan, which was striving for change and improvement.

This story is one of transformation, hope, and the tireless efforts of women who, in the hardest of circumstances, sought a way to build a better future.

A Light in the Darkness – a Cooperative story of success

Wazhma Abdulrahim Zai

In 2001, following the fall of the first Taliban regime, the sound of hopeful footsteps echoed through the weary and wounded land of Afghanistan. Afghan families, after years of exile and migration, were returning to their homeland. Yet, the shadows of past darkness still loomed over their lives. Many were in search of stable livelihoods and hope to support their families. In the midst of this, the Khorasan Cooperative, the first formal women's trade organization in Kabul, emerged as a warm and safe haven for women and young returnees.

Established in 1991, this organization began to flourish once again in the heart of the capital after years of absence. With a focus on the painful experiences of the past, the Khorasan Cooperative set out to create job and educational opportunities for women who no longer wanted to remain in the shadows. Women stepped into society with greater confidence, acquiring skills that could help them sustain their livelihoods.

Wazhma Abdulrahim Zai was one of these brave and determined women who seized this opportunity. After returning to Afghanistan, she anxiously sought a means to support her family. But fortune smiled on her; one of her mentors, recognizing her talent and perseverance, introduced her to the Khorasan Cooperative. With an iron will and a passion in her heart, she quickly secured a position within the organization.

Her journey began in the field of fashion design, but soon, through her dedication and relentless efforts, she became a key member of the Cooperative. Wazhma was no longer just a designer; she was a leader, a mentor, and an inspiration to other women. The Cooperative environment taught her how to not only enhance her technical skills but also make a meaningful impact in society.

During these transformations, Wazhma realized that many women at home possessed valuable embroidery and sewing skills that needed more recognition. With the help of these women, she created a space where they could work from their homes, enabling them to contribute to their families' income while still attending to their children and household responsibilities. This work model, particularly for widows and underprivileged women, provided a path to a better life.

Through her creativity and innovation, Wazhma paved the way for empowering these women. She soon joined the Women and Children's Rights Research Foundation and began her work as a journalist. Over seven years of collaboration, she attained various managerial positions and served as a trainer in educational programs across different ministries. By training over 300 employees, she became a prominent figure in Afghan society.

But her journey didn't end there. In 2014, Wazhma migrated to Canada, where she earned a bachelor's degree in international development and a master's in public policy and law. She is now working as an information analyst and immigration and settlement case manager at COSTI Immigrant Services.

In an interview with me, Wazhma enthusiastically recalled the Khorasan Cooperative. She spoke of the beautiful days of learning and the skills she had acquired. With pride, she described how she and the women she collaborated with were able to bring high-quality products to market and achieve great success. Remembering those moments filled her with joy, and her eyes shone brightly with happiness.

Wazhma Abdulrahim Zai sees this journey as a launchpad that enabled her to bring about significant changes in Afghan society as a women's rights activist. Her success story is just one of the hundreds that demonstrate how the Khorasan Cooperative, by creating a space for learning and growth, has empowered the women and youth of Afghanistan. The organization not only provided job opportunities but also served as a platform for personal and social development.

Wazhma and other women of this land have, with determination and resilience, written a story of strength and success that will remind future generations that no matter how deep the darkness, there is always a light ready to shine through.

Chapter 5
The fall of the government and Afghan women's struggles

The calm before the storm

Around two weeks before the fall of Kabul and Dr Najibullah's government and the formation of the Mujahideen, we began to sense the coming end. In the final days of April 1992, Kabul was filled with a calm before the storm. Even in the way women dressed, subtle changes began to appear. I remember the first time I went to the market in the Shahr-e-Naw area of Kabul, to buy food, a week before the arrival of the Mujahideen. I wore a spring coat, pants, and a chador/scarf, adapting to the sense of change that had begun to infiltrate our lives.

By the end of the fourth of May 1992, Kabul had fallen quietly with the arrival of various Mujahideen forces. Most provinces of Afghanistan had already been captured months earlier, and on the eighth of May 1992, the government of the People's Democratic Party collapsed, with military forces affiliated with the Jihadi groups entering Kabul from Jabal Saraj, Chahar Asyab, Surobi, and Maidan Shahr. The security belts around Kabul had been broken, and there were no longer any obstacles to the entry of armed groups. In such a situation, the outbreak of war seemed inevitable.

On the morning of the seventh of May 1992, Sibghatullah Mojaddedi, accompanied by a large caravan of members of the Transitional Council and dozens of Islamic party members, left Peshawar for Kabul. On the eighth of May, he entered Kabul, greeted by thousands of gunshots from the armed groups, and by five in the afternoon that day, he formally took power from the previous government. This transfer of power was ceremonial and symbolic. It was precisely on the eighth of May 1992 that the foundation of the People's Democratic Party government collapsed. Unfortunately, from the early morning of the eighth of May until the evening of that same day, government offices, military units, banks, universities, and schools were subjected to the largest and most unprecedented looting in the past century.

A memoir of bedridden days

For twenty days, I had not left my house and had only been watching events from my window. The people passing through the streets were unusual in appearance; many men with long hair and informal clothing. During the rule of the People's Democratic Party of Afghanistan, we became familiar with the random rocket fire and the atrocities that trapped thousands in our land. Through the news, we learned about the violence occurring in villages and forts, against men and women of the government. Now, our fate lay in their hands and we faced an uncertain future.

After twenty days, I went to the university wearing different clothes and a large scarf that covered half of my body to make my presence known. Classes were still suspended, and this reality seemed even more alarming. Everywhere was under the control of Mujahideen forces. During this time, women, as one of the vulnerable groups in society, bore the brunt of the Afghan civil war and suffered greatly.

Women faced even greater social restrictions. Some Mujahideen groups, especially the more radical ones, imposed limitations on their education, presence in public spaces, and jobs. Furthermore, women's education was impacted by restrictive decisions in some areas, and their studies and upbringing faced sanctions and social and cultural limitations.

The takeover of the Cooperative

In that dark and sorrowful era, Afghan women stood resiliently, with unparalleled courage and determination, enduring limitations and discrimination under the heavy shadows of cultural, social, and legal sanctions.

Every day in the urban landscape of Kabul, various stories unfolded; on one hand, life under the pressure of restrictions and grim, turbulent images, and on the other, the celebratory gunfire of the Mujahideen during their victories pierced the ears and transformed the atmosphere of the city at night.

With the sudden arrival of the Mujahideen at the cooperative office, all calmness and resilience had shattered. The place where women worked tirelessly to earn their livelihoods became a scene of fear and terror. Women, with trembling hands and hearts filled with dread, searched for a place to hide.

The Mujahideen, with cold and ruthless eyes, were looking for something to plunder. When they entered the office and realized it was merely a women's sewing cooperative, their anger and frustration still turned against us. Even this realization was not enough, as they ordered us to vacate the office. Despair and hopelessness engulfed the women, as they could no longer nurture their dreams of improvement and a bright future within those walls.

The Mujahideen seized the house because we had rented it from its owner, who lived abroad, and one of the commanders settled his family in the cooperative building. The day we were forced to leave the building was incredibly sorrowful and disheartening, as the place that served as a gathering for women and provided opportunities for them, especially for the breadwinners of families, no longer existed.

The takeover of the cooperative office was only the beginning of a dark and sorrowful era. The wars, spreading from house to house and from street to street, facilitated further migrations. In this dark period, hope for a better future for Afghan women remained alive, but it was accompanied by greater fear and anxiety.

Consequences of the Civil War

After the eighth of Swar 1992 and the rise of the Mujahideen, many past achievements were destroyed. Restrictions were imposed on mixed work and education for women and men, as well as on women's dress. The destruction of buildings belonging to some educational institutions caused many, many girls and women to be deprived of education and work.

The fourteen-year struggle of the Mujahideen against the former Soviet Union had ended in victory. However, the leaders of the jihadist parties had still not reached an agreement to form a provisional government. It was expected that the war in Afghanistan would come to an end, but the people, accustomed to political regime changes or what they referred to as "royal rotations," remained anxious, and many were fleeing Kabul for Pakistan and Iran. Many others still did not know what fate awaited them and what actions they should take. I was one of those lost individuals, bewildered and uncertain about what to do.

With the victory of the Mujahideen and the establishment of the Islamic State of Afghanistan, the war did not end. On April 25 of that same year, another war broke out in Kabul; a conflict that shook the capital under the fire of tanks and heavy artillery, an experience that the people of Afghanistan had not witnessed before in the twentieth century. This time, the war was between the Mujahideen factions and gradually took on an ethnic dimension. During this period, my family and I were still bewildered and lost, as the battlefronts grew hotter.

The internal wars displaced thousands from Afghanistan. Many people left the country for Iran, Pakistan, European countries, and other places to escape the reach of tanks, artillery, and bullets. These forced migrations were set to repeat over and over again.

Chapter 6
From challenges to new opportunities

Reflections on forced migration

Forced migration and human dispersion, as a historical and social phenomenon, have occurred throughout the world and have brought numerous consequences and damages. From personal experience some of the most significant problems resulting from forced migration include:
Leaving homelands and breaking ties: *Forced migrants are often compelled to leave their homeland due to war, political persecution, or racial discrimination. This migration not only results in the loss of their possessions and homes but can also lead to the severing of cultural and social ties and the experience of alienation.*
Physical and psychological hazards: *In the course of forced migration, individuals face physical and psychological dangers. They may encounter life-threatening situations in oceans, deserts, or dangerous areas. Additionally, experiences of fear, stress, and psychological trauma are common issues faced by forced migrants.*
Lack of resources and basic services: *Forced migrants may be relocated to areas with limited resources and inadequate basic services. This situation can lead to shortages of food, water, shelter, and healthcare, jeopardizing their health.*
Loss of family connections: *Forced migration can result in separation from family members and the loss of familial relationships. This issue can create internally displaced persons or international refugees and exacerbate the social isolation of migrants.*
Lack of access to education and employment: *Forced migrants may face challenges in accessing education and job opportunities due to irregular legal status and legal restrictions. This can lead to unemployment and prevent their children from receiving an education.*

Discrimination and prejudice: *Forced migrants may encounter discrimination and prejudice in their new place of residence. This can result in social isolation, deprivation of access to services and equal opportunities, and the emergence of racial and social disparities.*

Forced migration is typically regarded as a major humanitarian disaster and requires international attention to help address this issue and provide better conditions for forced migrants.

An unintended journey

Internal migration was an experience that I encountered unwillingly in my life. This difficult and challenging journey began with leaving my home in Kabul due to unpredictable circumstances. This sudden decision led me on an unplanned and unknown journey, which, as time went on, became heavier on my shoulders.

At first, feelings of urgency and discomfort overwhelmed me. I felt as though I no longer belonged to that environment. On one hand, losing all my acquaintances and friends, leaving my home, and starting a new life posed numerous challenges. On the other hand, these experiences brought about countless fears and doubts. However, over time, I gradually managed to turn this experience into an opportunity. During this journey, I met new cultures and people and learned new skills. The experience of migration transformed me into a more resilient and stronger person. It turned into a life story where every day presents new challenges and opportunities. Migration became an endless educational journey for me, where each moment offers a new chance for growth and advancement.

Although the experience of migration was a complex challenge filled with difficulties, the process caused the need to continually adapt; to new cultures and changes in living conditions which were indeed overwhelming but nevertheless, this experience also opened doors to new opportunities and experiences for me.

Two months after the Mujahideen government took power the chaotic and violent conditions in the city and its streets had not diminished. We decided anyway to travel from Kabul to Mazar-e-Sharif. It was a hard day. The sun was slowly shining on the horizon, but nothing could ease the heaviness in our hearts. We faced the difficulty of finding a flight to Mazar-e-Sharif, which though very limited during those days, was a sign of hope for continuing life in these critical conditions.

When we arrived at the Khwaja Rawash Kabul airport, a heartbreaking scene awaited us. The coffins of martyrs, young men who had sacrificed their lives in meaningless internal conflicts, were lined up neatly for transportation to their respective provinces. These coffins, like precious but dark jewels, represented the heavy toll of war. Each one carried an untold story of love, hope, and unfulfilled dreams.

I found myself staring at the coffins. In that moment, I felt a deep sorrow enveloping my entire being. My eyes were fixed on those of my companions, and in our gazes, I could see despair and confusion. An unclear and ambiguous future loomed ahead of us, and it felt as if a cold wind from the heart of war and destruction was blowing toward us.

These images vividly illustrated the painful reality of war and its impact on people's lives. Despite all the difficulties, we knew we had to think about continuing our journey. In the heart of darkness, there was a small glimmer of hope that pushed us forward. And as the plane prepared for take-off, despite all this pain, I looked at the coffins and told myself that we must move forward for them and for the unfulfilled dreams that remain on the ground. Life goes on, and we too must hold on to that hope.

Cultural diversity and opportunities in Balkh province

Upon arriving in Mazar-e-Sharif, we were welcomed at the home of a relative who had been living there for years. We are endlessly grateful for their hospitality and kindness. Mazar-e-Sharif is one of the important and historic provinces in Afghanistan, known as the "City of Mola Ali." The shrine of Imam Ali (AS) in this city serves as an historical, religious, and pilgrimage attraction for Muslims from around the world. The local markets, historic mosques, and sacred sites in this city immerse travellers in a world of cultural and spiritual beauty.

The people of Balkh province invite travellers to experience a culturally and historically distinct journey with their rich culture and hospitality. During my earlier life, one of my heartfelt wishes was to visit the shrine of Shah-e-Olia, that place in the world which, through the grace and will of God, is filled with values and great dignity. Interestingly, just a few days before the realization of this wish, I saw myself in a dream visiting Shah-e-Olia – the dream now became a reality.

In my prayers, I asked for peace and tranquillity to prevail in our beloved country. My wish remained that by accepting divine will and adhering to high ethical principles, we can reach a place where all individuals in society live together with respect and love for one another. The journey to the shrine of Shah-e-Olia was not only a religious experience but also a strategy for better understanding the true path of life. I hope still that this wish for peace and tranquillity becomes a reality through the efforts and determination of all, and that our country progresses towards transformation and growth with the light of divine guidance.

As days passed and time went on, we realized that the flow of migrants, especially from Kabul and other insecure provinces to the city of Mazar-e-Sharif had increased. Every day, groups of migrants entered the city, all dressed in limited clothing and carrying belongings that indicated they were not in a good economic situation. Typically, the male family members would come to the city first to seek day labour jobs and secure the livelihood of themselves and their families.

We were all in search of a suitable place to stay during uncertain and calm times. The city of Mazar-e-Sharif, under the rule of Abdul Rashid Dostum, was like a covered shadow, supportive and hopeful for people from insecure areas and provinces who could find job opportunities and experience a better life without worrying about war and armed conflicts.

In our initial search, we found a room connected to a small storage area, part of which we used as a kitchen. This room was located in a shared courtyard with the house owner, who had a traditional toilet in one corner of the yard. We had to draw water from a well that was hand-pulled with a wheel, a completely new experience for us but gradually providing us with more basic tools to start a new life.

Unfamiliarity with the environment, adapting to living conditions, traditions and values, cultural and local differences, and establishing effective communication with local people who differed from what we knew were challenges we faced. Moreover, the lack of access to cultural resources, education, and cultural opportunities was also a significant challenge we struggled with. Even the different climatic conditions of the city of Mazar-e-Sharif, which has a hot and dry climate, compared to Kabul, regarded as a cold region, had created significant challenges.

By deepening our understanding of cultural and social differences, we were able to adapt ourselves to the environmental conditions of Mazar-e-Sharif and establish effective communication with the local people.

The educational opportunities for the displaced were seen as a valuable and vital in the lives of families. Despite the challenges arising from the war, the opportunity of continuing education in Mazar-e-Sharif was possible. In this regard, my children benefited from such opportunities – my son joined the twelfth grade, while my daughter temporarily joined the eleventh grade at school. My son was able to take a positive step towards continuing his education in the field of law by successfully passing the entrance exam at the end of the academic year. Measures taken in the field of education and training under General Dostum's rule allowed school and university teachers as well as government employees in various fields to find acceptance. Additionally, non-governmental and international organizations soon became involved and provided humanitarian assistance to migrants.

My story of migration, entrepreneurship, and transformation in Mazar-e-Sharif

During my migration, when unemployment cast a heavy shadow over my life, I decided not to surrender to fate. Instead of sitting idle, I found a way to change my situation with the small amount of capital I had. Renting a small shop in Mazar-e-Sharif to sell imported second-hand clothing marked the beginning of a journey full of effort and hope. I started this business through my son, who helped me in his free time. His support and collaboration not only turned this small business into a source of income for the family but, in a very real sense, transformed my life.

But life is always changing. After some time, with the improvement of the security situation in Kabul, we decided to return home. This return was filled with hope and aspiration, but it also meant we had to close our shop in Mazar-e-Sharif. My son stayed there to continue his studies at Balkh University, while I returned to Kabul.

At that moment, I decided to continue on the path I had started; to enter cooperative work and look for new opportunities to improve the economic situation of my family and other women who, like me, were searching for a chance to change their lives. From the very beginning, I knew that I was not the only one struggling with the hardships of life. Many women in this land, with hearts full of dreams and hope, are still trapped in the shadows of poverty and unemployment. Many of them are searching for an opportunity to stand on their own feet and provide for their families, but the difficult conditions and a society that often assigns limited roles to women makes their path incredibly challenging.

I decided that not only would I move toward change myself, but I would also extend a helping hand to other women in need. At this point in my journey, I thought about establishing a cooperative project for women in need, a place where they could not only find jobs but prove their capabilities and, with their own hands, build a brighter future.

This project would not only provide them with an opportunity to break free from limitations but also create a space for learning and personal growth. For many of these women, working is not just an economic necessity but a way to free themselves from the chains of injustice and social constraints. I came to believe that when women are given the opportunity, they can not only change their own lives but also build a better society.

With enthusiasm and hope, I launched this project, giving women from villages and various cities the chance to step into this new world. Women who once felt they had no place in the world around them could now participate in these projects with confidence and courage. Day by day, the number of women joining this path grew, and this was just the beginning.

This was the start of a journey for women who had grown tired of the dark and difficult days of life. Now, with eyes full of hope for the future, they stood together to create a new tomorrow. On this journey, nothing was more precious to me than seeing their smiles and hearing their stories of success. This was not only a transformation in my own life, but also a change in the world of women who never believed they could overcome their pain and limitations.

Journey under the shadow of violence

Unfortunately, it wasn't long before violent clashes between different factions of the Mujahideen began again in Kabul. These groups became fiercely opposed to each other, dividing the neighbourhoods of the city among themselves. Heavy fighting affected several areas of Kabul, and tensions reached their peak. This not only resulted in the deaths of many innocent people, including children, youth, and adults, but also led to the widespread destruction of the city, forcing people to migrate from one area to another due to relentless dangers.

We also fled from Shahr-e Naw, which was under heavy attack, to the Taimani area, seeking refuge in the home of our relatives. In the house that belonged to my late father-in-law, many other relatives had also taken shelter. Despite all the hardships, we sometimes thought about funny things or reminisced about peaceful times. Everyone, despite having little, would generously offer what they had with open hearts and kind spirits. We shared how our dreams were gradually being lost, one by one, in the face of the discouraging winds of time.

During this time, we realized that the city of Mazar-e-Sharif too was still facing issues of insecurity, civil war, and military attacks. Our concern grew, as my son, who was studying at Balkh University and living in the university dormitory, was caught in these complex and difficult circumstances, and we had no way to communicate with him directly.

We heard that the living conditions for students at the university were deteriorating. This increased our worry. Therefore, I decided to go to Mazar-e-Sharif and bring my son back to Kabul with me. Given the political situation and my husband's duties, traveling to Mazar-e-Sharif through Kabul was likely to be fraught with difficulties due to the control of various groups. As a result, I decided to travel overland with my brother-in-law using provincial buses towards Mazar-e-Sharif. A decision made due to the closure of airports in Afghanistan.

On the morning of our departure, dressed in a burqa, I set off with my brother-in-law, stopping briefly in Pul-e-Khumri city on our way to Mazar-e-Sharif. The journey toward Mazar-e-Sharif revealed signs of battle and destruction from factional wars at every turn. The ruins, destroyed tanks, and armed checkpoints were all indicators that war had passed through this area. Everywhere we went, we encountered many questions and challenges from various armed groups, where even the slightest mistake could lead to a person's disappearance into the shadows, leaving no trace of their existence.

During our journey, we had several encounters with different armed factions. Fortunately, nothing happened to us, but it is very difficult to describe the frightening and grim atmosphere surrounding us. The armed individuals we faced were utterly terrifying. The scenes we witnessed along the way were constant reminders of horror and fear.

Every moment we spent on this journey told a bitter story of war and destruction. The psychological and physical effects of these experiences impacted many aspects of people's lives. In this narrative of history, the physical and emotional wounds of the people are highlighted. This journey was not just a geographical one; it was a profound exploration of the wounds inflicted on society and humanity by war. Every step we took was accompanied by dread and fear, and every encounter with armed groups reminded us of bitter tales of insecurity. Would we be able to reach Mazar-e-Sharif, or would this path lead us into further troubles?

A woman's story from danger to power

Reaching the city of Mazar-e-Sharif was a significant goal. With perseverance through numerous hardships, we arrived in Pul-e-Khumri that evening. We spent the night at the home of one of our relatives, who resided there permanently. We were supposed to leave for Mazar-e-Sharif the next day. The atmosphere was tense. When we went to the bus station, we sadly realized that travellers were not being allowed to depart. With great disappointment, which no words could fully capture, we returned to our relatives' home.

Although, we were to stay at our relatives' house for an indefinite period, they showed us endless hospitality and we were in good living conditions. They encouraged us and sometimes even organized fun games to help us forget our pain and suffering.

Finally, after four days of waiting, we heard that a minibus was heading towards Mazar-e-Sharif. Filled with joy, we went to the station but were deeply saddened to learn that groups were pulling young men off the buses and taking them away, possibly to participate in fighting or for reasons unknown to us. This made me anxious, and I didn't want my brother-in-law to risk his life. My brother-in-law decided to stay in the city of Pul-e-Khumri, and I decided to travel to Mazar-e-Sharif alone. With a heavy heart, I found a seat in the middle of the bus at the station. Everyone standing in the minibus seemed to be carrying the burden of a hopeless fate, but I was determined to keep my heart filled with hope until I reached Mazar-e-Sharif to rescue my son.

The bus started moving towards its destination. After half an hour, we reached a place called Cheshmeh Shir. A few people were standing by the roadside and signalled the driver to stop. While I thought they might want to board the bus, one of them, with his face covered and only his eyes visible, gave the driver's assistant a hard slap. Then, another man took the fare money out of his pocket and, pointing his gun while threatening the others, demanded that everyone pay them ten thousand Afghanis. They started from the front row. A man who had no money begged for mercy, but they responded mercilessly and collected all the valuable belongings the passengers had before leaving.

This story speaks of the great challenges Afghan women endure during internal conflicts, especially when they find themselves in difficult and dangerous situations. At any moment, I could have faced a situation that threatened my life and honour, but thanks to God, they didn't ask me for anything. They didn't even realize that I was traveling alone without a male guardian. In such times, being alone can be a serious threat, but I managed to hide this fact from their gaze.

In fact, inside the bus no one noticed that I was alone. I sat in the first row next to another woman who was with her young son. Her son was sitting on the small seat beside us, as the bus didn't have enough space for everyone to sit. All the men were standing in the middle of the bus, paying no attention to comfort or position, with only one goal in mind: to reach the city of Mazar-e-Sharif through these dangerous roads.

This unwanted and terrifying experience gave me a deep understanding of the injustices and challenges faced as a woman traveling alone on the road to Mazar-e-Sharif. Each moment could have turned into a disaster, but I emerged from this ordeal unscathed. Perhaps it was due to luck, patience, perseverance, and maybe a little bit of hope and God's grace that helped me through.

Amidst this darkness and fear, the light of hope continued to shine within me. I knew that every step I took painted a picture of resilience and steadfastness. As a woman, I was not only confronting physical challenges but also battling the weight of history and my society's culture. This journey would shape me into a stronger and more independent woman.

In the end, when I reached my destination, I realized that I had completed not only a physical journey but also a spiritual one. With every heartbeat and every breath, the voice within me declared that I was the hero of my own story. This journey was not just to Mazar-i-Sharif but also to my own heart and soul. There, I learned that my femininity was not a weakness, but rather a source of strength against all challenges and hardships.

Just when I thought the dangers were behind us, we suddenly encountered another armed group along the way. With the sound of gunfire and threatening shouts, everyone's hearts began to race. The driver was forced to stop the bus. In that moment, we all fell into a deadly silence. Fear and terror were clearly visible on the faces of the passengers, especially in my own eyes.

The armed group, with their harsh faces and weapons in hand, ordered the driver to give them some fuel from the vehicle's reserve tank. While the driver, with a trembling voice and full of apologies, explained that if he gave them the fuel, he wouldn't be able to take us to our destination, fear pierced through my heart like a deep dagger. Would they show mercy to me as well? As a lone woman among them, was I safe?

The armed group's severe threats brought the driver to his knees. With eyes full of fear, struggling to maintain his composure, he reluctantly gave them some of the reserve fuel. This moment placed a new burden on our journey.

I, as a lone woman who had managed to keep myself hidden from others' eyes until that moment, felt my heart pounding heavily and my whole-body trembling. Perhaps my face had turned pale. The fear that if the bus ran out of fuel, what would happen next engulfed me completely. What would I do alone in this dangerous path where I saw nothing but fear and horror? Could these passengers, these seemingly hardened men, protect me?

Although the other passengers might have been good people, at that moment, they all seemed to have turned harsh. Their worried and serious expressions made me feel utterly vulnerable. In that instant, thoughts flooded my mind: Why did I embark on this dangerous journey? I recalled the days when we had lived a life of dignity and respect. Why had everything turned so brutal and merciless so suddenly?

These conflicting and sorrowful feelings weighed heavily on my heart. I felt as if I were trapped in a real hell, where my hopes and dreams were imprisoned like a caged bird. In that darkness, despair was so overwhelming that it felt as if I could no longer breathe. All

I had left at that moment were the cold tears streaming down my cheeks.

But this was not the end. Unfortunately, an hour later, further along the road, another group blocked our bus. Again, my heart pounded violently, and I felt that all my hopes were at risk. I could hear their shouts, and my hands were trembling uncontrollably. But suddenly, with a daring move, the driver found an opportunity and sped forward. It was as if life and death were in his hands.

As the armed groups fired at us from behind, the sound of bullets, like thunder in the clear daytime sky, filled me with sheer terror. The bus windows shook, and I screamed inwardly, "Oh God, please save us!" The only thing I could see were the anxious faces of other passengers, sunk deep in fear and panic, mirroring my own.

Fortunately, we weren't harmed physically, but my heartbeat continued to race intensely. After these horrifying experiences, I felt a mix of emotions. Initially, the fear and worry from the threats and danger tore at my heart, and then a deeper sense of unease settled within me.

This experience became a bitter turning point. Questions went through my mind again. Why were we placed in such a situation? What had brought us to this point? Under the bright daylight, I remembered the days gone by, when my life was filled with peace and happiness. But now, everything had changed. I felt as if I were caught in a dangerous game, and at any moment, my life could come to an end.

These unanswered questions swirled in my mind, and the tears flowed uncontrollably down my cheeks. I found myself fighting not only external enemies but also my own inner fears and despair. In those moments, hope and courage flickered like a flame in my heart, and I resolved never to surrender. This journey was not just a physical challenge, but a deep internal struggle with my inner self.

We finally arrived at district Kulm (Tashkurghan) Samangan city. The driver, with a satisfied smile, said: "This is General Dostum's territory; from here on, you don't need to worry about any danger." I felt a bit relieved. When we reached the gate of Mazar-e-Sharif, the signs of a heavy rainstorm from a few hours earlier had altered the streets' appearance. A small road leading towards the Karte-Solh area was completely flooded. I had been silent throughout the journey, but at that moment, I said, "Stop! I'll get off here." Without paying attention to the murky waters beneath my feet, I stepped forward.

After a long and eventful journey, I was happy to have arrived safely in Mazar-e-Sharif, despite enduring many hardships. I was eager to find out about my son. I reached the house of a family friend, where we had lived for a while. The door was open, and I entered the courtyard with weary steps. Each step reminded me of the dangers I had overcome. Upon entering the courtyard, I saw surprise on everyone's faces. They asked me how I had managed to get here despite all the road and air routes being closed and the dangers I had faced.

I quickly asked about my son, but they told me they had no news and that he hadn't contacted them yet. At that same moment, a neighbour's son had already informed his classmate that his mother had arrived, and my child rushed toward me, filled with joy. However, my unintended journey marked the beginning of a new life for me in Mazar-e-Sharif. I had no means of communication to let my family in Kabul know about my well-being or whether my journey had proceeded safely.

Towards family and community self-sufficiency

After twenty days my son and I sat together anxiously, unaware of what was happening. Suddenly, I saw my husband passing by the window. Fortunately, he had arrived in Mazar-e-Sharif that day. His concern over my lack of news drove him to undertake the risky journey to this city. This moment reminded me of how important and valuable it is to have each other's support during difficult times.

Alongside this reunion, we now carried the pain of other unexpected events in our lives. Our separation from our daughter created a sea of unexpressed emotions in our hearts. During those days, every moment felt like a longing in our home, while the winter winds of Kabul swirled around every corner of the city.

Any news we received about our daughter painted a vague and concerning picture of her life and that of our other relatives. From afar, with limited information, we tried to stay updated on her well-being. However, security restrictions continually raised the walls between us. Despite severe security issues on the highways between Kabul and other provinces, after two years of effort and struggle, I was finally able to bring my daughter, who was living with her grandparents in Kabul, to Mazar-e-Sharif and enrol her in the Faculty of Literature at Balkh University after passing the entrance exam.

During our stay in Mazar-e-Sharif, I proudly witnessed the significant achievements of my children. My son earned his bachelor's degree in law from Balkh University, and my daughter, with hard work and dedication, continued her studies in the second year of the History Department in the Faculty of Literature. These were moments filled with pride and joy for my family, moments that were the result of our relentless efforts.

Millions of other families across the country had joined us in the province and experienced similar sorrow and hardships. This difficult period not only tested our capacities but also served as a profound lesson in striving to defend deep human and social values.

Despite our new life being full of challenges and significant changes, the initial days in our new home brought fresh air into this new space. Despite all the newness and differences, a sense of home gradually grew in our hearts.

My children were busy with pursuing education whereas I, on the other hand, was still searching for my life's path. Questions lingered in my mind: What path should I choose? Should I look for a specific job and profession, or should I seize every opportunity that came my way? As I looked out the window at the street, a world of possibilities and challenges awaited us.

Every day, I sought greater motivation in our new city. I wanted to carve a path for myself and bring colour and flavour to our new life. Decisions were uncertain, but I was certain that the more I pursued my desires and aspirations, the deeper the connection I would feel in this new home.

With eager enthusiasm, I searched for job opportunities to enhance my experiences in language and literature gained from my education at Kabul University. Although this academic experience was primarily theoretical, the skills I acquired from the business sector reflected my skills across various fields. My experiences, especially in management and economics gained through collaboration with the Khorasan Cooperative in Kabul, allowed me not only to deeply understand business concepts but also to develop suitable strategies to face market challenges and transformations.

Given my extensive experience in both theory and practice, I sought an opportunity to offer innovative and effective solutions to grow and develop handicrafts for women and young girls, directly and indirectly benefiting their families. My aim was to make a meaningful impact in supporting vulnerable women, especially migrants who had come to Mazar-e-Sharif from various provinces due to internal conflicts. Through organizing workshops and training sessions, I aimed to encourage them towards self-sufficiency and the creation of business opportunities.

Having always placed great importance on serving and understanding the needs of individuals in the community, I decided not to join Balkh University as a temporary lecturer. Instead, I aimed to leverage my experiences in small and medium enterprise programs in both times of war and peace to establish an effective program. This effort was focused on addressing social priorities and playing an active role in supporting the neediest members of the community.

With limited capital, I rented a three-room apartment in the Karte Solh area, district seven of Mazar-e-Sharif, and established a branch office for the Khorasan Trade Cooperative. My goal in these efforts was to provide professional skills training, organize production programs, and raise awareness on various issues, including the role of women in local decision-making in the seventh district of Mazar-e-Sharif.

Next, we spread the word through mosque loudspeakers, local representatives, and prominent women, inviting local women to participate in the public meeting at the Khorasan Cooperative office. The opening of such an office in Mazar-e-Sharif was a completely new phenomenon. Many women eagerly visited this centre, where the goals and programs were introduced to them. Young women registered for sewing and cutting courses. Those skilled in embroidery, woven garment production, carpet weaving, and rug making received raw materials for their products, creating them in their homes. In return, they received wages, and the products were sent to the centre. At this centre, products were packaged, priced, marketed, and sold. This process created a sustainable production flow, leading to visible development and progress.

Most beneficiaries of the program were school dropouts, widows, impoverished women, and those who were the breadwinners of their families, particularly women who had migrated due to internal conflicts and suffered from life in refugee camps, such as the Kamaz camp, which lacked adequate facilities.

In these challenging conditions, the school dropout program played a vital role in improving the living conditions of these vulnerable groups. This program acted as a bridge between women and educational resources, social support, and job opportunities.

Some of the program's objectives included:

Education and training: Providing scientific and technical training to school dropouts so they could learn the necessary skills to enter the job market.

Social support: Creating a supportive environment for girls to strengthen them emotionally, socially, and economically, making them feel valued by the community.

Employment promotion: Offering suitable job opportunities based on the abilities and interests of women and young girls.

Economic support: Providing financial support through work, especially to impoverished and widowed women, so they could meet their basic needs.

Continuing education: Creating opportunities for girls to continue their education and enhance their knowledge to become effective members of society in the future.

Such programs provided better opportunities for women and girls living in migration conditions to develop their skills and increase their awareness, moving from a difficult situation toward an independent and successful life. These programs not only aided the girls but also helped the community pay greater attention to significant issues like women's empowerment and the reduction of social gaps.

Opening of the Khorasan Cooperative for the economic empowerment of women

When many people migrated to Mazar-e-Sharif due to the internal conflicts and factional wars in Afghanistan, especially from Kabul, the demand for relief, humanitarian, and economic services significantly increased. Governmental and non-governmental organizations, as well as international bodies, implemented various programs to address the needs of these migrants. These programs included education, healthcare, and economic support, which substantially improved the living conditions of migrants.

In this context, I established the *Khorasan Cooperative* in Mazar-e-Sharif to assist women affected by war and migration. This agency was specifically designed to economically empower women, aiming to support migrant and vulnerable women and improve their livelihoods by creating job opportunities and offering vocational training.

The programs of this centre were innovatively designed to address the real needs of the migrant and affected communities. The focus of these programs was on professional skills training, such as sewing, carpet weaving, and knitting, so that women could use these skills to generate income and become self-sufficient. The centre not only provided training but also supplied the necessary raw materials for them to produce goods.

With continuous efforts, this agency was warmly welcomed by the people and became recognized as a successful model in women's economic empowerment. Both migrants and locals eagerly attended the centre and benefited from its programs. This project had a significant impact on improving the conditions of affected women and became one of the most successful social and economic initiatives in Mazar-i-Sharif.

Building connections – *Conference on the Economic & Social Situation of Afghan Women*

In 1994, I participated in a conference titled "The Economic and Social Situation of Women in Afghanistan," held at Balkh University in the city of Mazar-e-Sharif. As one of the professors from Kabul University who had relocated to the city due to migration, I was invited to represent the Khorasan Cooperative. This was an incredibly enriching experience, as it provided me with the opportunity to share my thoughts and suggestions with other participants.

In addition to actively participating in the discussions, I was given the responsibility of organizing a handicraft exhibition. Participating in this conference and exhibition offered a unique opportunity to showcase the products of the Khorasan Cooperative. The event was attended by prominent women of Balkh province, including university professors and heads of governmental and non-governmental organizations. I was honoured to be one of the speakers at the conference, where I was given a chance to deliver a brief statement about the economic and social conditions of women, as well as discuss the activities of the cooperative, which had recently opened its first branch in Mazar-e-Sharif.

As the conference progressed, with the formation of working groups to assess challenges and propose solutions, an atmosphere filled with hope and collaboration emerged. Amidst this enthusiasm, the appreciation of my efforts and the value of the cooperative work I had initiated – entirely funded by myself – was deeply encouraging. The sincere understanding from the women present, including Samantha Reynolds, now known as Samantha Leader, head of the UN-Habitat office in Mazar-e-Sharif, was especially heartening. She symbolized love and loyalty to Afghanistan, demonstrating unwavering commitment to supporting various programs, particularly those focused on youth and women. With her exceptional character and friendly spirit, she fostered a warm and welcoming environment that aligned perfectly with Afghan culture and traditions. She made every decision in consultation with local staff, which allowed her to deeply understand the real needs and challenges of the people.

I must also acknowledge Nancy Dupree, an American researcher, archaeologist, historian, and renowned scholar on Afghanistan. She recognized the importance of cooperative efforts and often spoke passionately about these initiatives during conferences and group gatherings. Nancy, who passed away at the age of 90 in Afghanistan, dedicated more than half a century of her life – 53 years – to extensive research, academic work, and promoting tourism in the country. Even in her final moments, she remained with the people of Afghanistan, showing her endless love and dedication to this land. Her legacy lives on in the hearts of many, and her contributions to understanding and preserving Afghanistan's history and culture will never be forgotten.

Meeting Rahela Jan Hashim Sidiqi for the first time at this conference was a valuable and inspiring experience. At that time, before joining UN-Habitat, she was working as an employee at the United Nations High Commissioner for Refugees (UNHCR), bringing with her valuable experiences and insights. Getting to know her was like discovering a hidden treasure of knowledge and virtue. Additionally, she had a deep interest in cooperative activities in Mazar-e-Sharif. After she joined UN-Habitat, collaborating with her was an unforgettable experience for me. The stories from that period are so rich and inspiring that they could perhaps fill an entire book.

Overall, these consultative meetings not only allowed me to share my experiences with others, but also, through a blend of cultural and professional diversity, fostered valuable exchanges and enhanced both individual and collective awareness.

Over the course of six months, a large number of visitors continuously came to observe the activities of the cooperative.

These visits were the result of the efforts of me, an Afghan woman who, through self-reliance and without relying on foreign aid, implemented a program in Mazar-e-Sharif. The goal of this program was to assist people in difficult circumstances and have a positive impact on the community.

Given that the social programs designed by the leadership team at UN-Habitat seemed aligned with the cooperative's activities, I was asked to join this organization as an employee. This opportunity allowed me to serve as one of the field executives, helping to expand Habitat's social programs under the name "Women's Community Forums" and contribute to social development in all areas of Mazar-e-Sharif.

Accepting this opportunity meant serving the community for me – not as a temporary resident, but as someone committed to improving the conditions of the city. I hoped that every area of our city would benefit from this program and its focus on social development. This decision reflected the belief that through solidarity and collective effort, we could bring progress and improvement to our community, achieving great outcomes from small steps.

In the same year, the United Nations Human Settlements Programme (UN-Habitat) launched an innovative initiative in the city of Mazar-e-Sharif – *Poverty Eradication and Community Empowerment* (PEACE). The primary objective of this program was to establish sustainable, multi-purpose community Forums (CFs) in neighbourhoods, aimed at improving access to economic, educational, and social services for both men and women across diverse communities.

This initiative was introduced with the goal of combating poverty through active community participation, strengthening local capacities, and promoting equal opportunities to enhance the quality of life, particularly in vulnerable communities. As part of this program, projects such as the establishment of social forums were implemented to foster local solidarity, deliver integrated services, and increase the effective participation of women and men in the process of sustainable development.

It is with deep appreciation that I recall the pivotal role played by Samantha Leader, UN-Habitat's Senior Technical Advisor for Afghanistan, during a critical period in the country's recovery. Through unwavering commitment and profound cultural sensitivity, she worked tirelessly with her team to design and implement impactful social development programs grounded in deep respect for Afghan traditions.

Samantha redefined social development as a movement of peacebuilders — messengers of hope dedicated to restoring lives and strengthening communities. Her leadership embodied not only strategic foresight but also deep empathy and genuine solidarity with the people of Afghanistan during times of great hardship.

Facing the challenges of growing a community organization

In 1995, when I began working as a field officer for the UN-Habitat community development program, I was thrust into a world of heavy responsibilities and challenges. With compassion and a deep motivation that came from within, along with the experience I had gained over the years, I stood resolutely against the difficulties, initiating projects aimed at improving the living conditions of the people in Mazar-e-Sharif in a purposeful and practical way.

Our team, driven by boundless motivation and tireless effort, successfully established ten Community Forums across ten districts in Mazar-e-Sharif. These achievements reflect not only our team's commitment and capability but also symbolize our dedication and determination to enhance the community's quality of life.

During this period, despite numerous challenges and obstacles, we successfully established ten Community Forums (CFs) across ten districts of Mazar-e-Sharif over nearly five years. To ensure the sustainability of these CFs, we founded a central organization known as the Community Forum Development Organization (CFDO).

This organization, established in collaboration with UN-Habitat, actively works towards self-sufficiency and plays a significant role in strengthening and supporting the forums. Alongside establishing the CFs, we implemented various empowerment and sustainable development projects aimed at enhancing community resilience and capacity. The positive impact of our initiatives in Mazar-e-Sharif has since spread all across the country, demonstrating the effectiveness and adaptability of our approach.

The inspiring journeys of women in Mazar-e-Sharif

Reflecting on my time working with the women of Mazar-e-Sharif fills me with pride and countless memories. The idea of creating a Community Forum (CF) was uncharted territory, especially in a region where the concept of shared responsibility and local empowerment was both novel and, initially, met with understandable hesitation. People were unfamiliar with the notion that they could actively shape the development of their communities. Building this awareness and helping them see the impact of their contributions was both a challenge and a rewarding journey.

From the beginning, the aim of the CF was clear: to bring people together, particularly women, to empower them with the tools and knowledge to drive change. Yet, encouraging women to participate in the forums, to voice their needs, and to realize their capacity to influence decisions wasn't easy. I remember one of the first meetings vividly – a modest gathering of local women who were, at first, more reserved. They listened cautiously, uncertain of how this forum would directly affect their lives. But slowly, as we shared stories of empowerment and small successes from nearby communities, I began to see curiosity spark in their eyes.

One woman, named Fatima, stands out in my memory. She was a single mother with little formal education, yet a natural leader in her neighbourhood. Initially hesitant, she attended a CF meeting out of curiosity. Over time, she began to see how the forum could address the needs of her community. She led discussions about healthcare, child education, and even sanitation, rallying the women around her. Fatima's transformation inspired others, and soon, she had mobilized a group of women determined to improve their circumstances. The CF became their platform to share ideas, make plans, and hold each other accountable.

These small but meaningful steps started to ripple outwards, gradually transforming the community. The women developed a sense of ownership, taking pride in the changes they were making. They started addressing not only personal and family matters but also broader issues affecting the entire community, becoming trusted voices within their neighbourhoods.

Seeing the women of Mazar-e-Sharif take charge of their futures has been incredibly fulfilling. Each story, each step forward, and each success shared in our CF meetings reminded me that, despite the initial difficulties, this work was crucial. The impact of these forums has spread well beyond Mazar-e-Sharif, reaching communities all over the country and igniting the same spirit of resilience and empowerment in countless others.

Looking back, I'm humbled by the strength of the women I worked with and their courage in embracing new ideas. Our work together not only transformed communities but, for me, solidified a lifelong commitment to fostering change in partnership with those most impacted by it.

An example of Community Participation – Construction of a drinking-water well

In one of the neighbourhoods of Mazar-e-Sharif, a community gathering was held to discuss the construction of a drinking water well, which turned into a vibrant and significant event. Local elders, residents, government representatives, and the mosque's imam gathered, demonstrating the people's commitment to solving a fundamental issue.

As a local employee responsible for women's integration programs, I attended the gathering alongside Habitat employees who managed technical aspects of irrigation. Our goal was to address the issue at hand. In this large assembly, everyone shared their opinions and ideas. The diversity of views showcased the community's ability to negotiate, unify, and engage in significant urban matters.

The crisis among residents revolved around constructing a drinking water well for the mosque. The key question was whether the well should be placed inside or outside the mosque. Most attendees, due to their deep connection to this sacred place, eagerly advocated for the well to be dug inside. However, the absence of women as effective representatives was raised as a significant concern, as women play a crucial role in managing daily water usage. Additionally, the mosque is a space for ablution and the five daily prayers, making it challenging for women to enter freely.

Initially, the proposal to dig the well inside the mosque faced mixed reactions. Upon closer examination, it became clear that women's opinions needed to be respectfully considered in this decision-making process. Some local elders, who believed women had no role in this matter, presented a considerable challenge. However, despite logical discussions, it was shown that women's perspectives and participation in this community meeting were considered worthless by the men.

After lengthy discussions, the elders ultimately agreed that women's voices should also be heard in the meeting. Their presence and strong arguments led to a decision that would allow everyone easy access to the well water. Women courageously participated as representatives of their community, providing detailed justifications for their stance. Ultimately, a wise decision was made to construct the drinking water well outside the mosque. This decision ensured that women could benefit from the well at any time, reflecting respect for the needs and wishes of all community members. It also facilitated easy access to water for all passersby, regardless of gender, since the mosque area is primarily for prayer and ablution, making it less accessible for women.

This experience highlights the importance of listening to all community members and actively involving them in urban decisions. This gathering not only exemplified coordination and solidarity within the community but also marked a new beginning for forming joint and sustainable decisions for the future of the city.

Reflections on the benefits of listening

This story of constructing a water well illustrates the coordination system within the community. Different individuals have come together to address a common issue: the establishment of a drinking water well for the local mosque. This gathering, which included local elders, residents, government representatives, local employees, and women who play a significant role in water consumption, exemplifies the resolution of a social problem through tolerance, understanding, the elimination of gender conflict, and the prevention of social disputes. This approach highlights solidarity and cooperation among community members and underscores the importance of respecting diverse viewpoints.

Throughout this process, various challenges and conflicts emerged, necessitating negotiation, logical discourse, and ultimately, coordination to reach shared decisions. This system emphasizes the significance of listening to all segments of society, resolving conflicts, and integrating different opinions to achieve a balanced decision.

The outcome of this process was the selection of an appropriate location for the construction of the drinking water well, considering the needs and desires of all community members, especially acknowledging the vital role of women involved in this matter. This reflects sustainability and harmony in urban decision-making. It underscores the importance of active participation by individuals in community decisions and the establishment of coordination to address issues.

The role of the adaptation program for women and local technical staff from the Habitat office is clearly highlighted in resolving the crisis related to the construction of the drinking water well. This experience demonstrates the importance of listening to all segments of society, the active participation of women, and the coordination necessary for solving community issues. This process can serve as a successful model for community development and empowerment programs.

An example of Community Participation – Promoting Afghan women's handicrafts

To promote marketing and showcase the products produced by the women of Mazar-e-Sharif, I also participated in an official trip to an international exhibition in Islamabad, Pakistan. During the exhibition we were able to highlight the remarkable craftsmanship and skills of the women artisans from Mazar-e-Sharif. Our booth featured a wide array of handmade products, including traditional embroidery, handwoven carpets, jewellery, and other decorative items that reflected the rich cultural heritage of Afghanistan. The aim was not only to promote these goods but also to introduce the broader international community to the creative potential and resilience of Afghan women.

The exhibition proved to be a significant platform for networking and establishing business connections. Our participation caught the attention of various international buyers and non-governmental organizations who expressed interest in supporting the initiative. Several products were successfully sold, and long-term orders were negotiated, providing a boost to the women's cooperatives back home. This exposure also enabled us to learn about new trends, quality standards, and packaging techniques, which we later integrated into the production process to meet international demands.

More importantly, the exhibition became a symbol of empowerment for the women involved. By showcasing their work on a global stage, we challenged stereotypes and demonstrated that Afghan women are not just survivors of conflict but active contributors to their community's economic and social development.

The experience invigorated the spirit of the Community Forums, as members felt a renewed sense of purpose and pride in their work.

After returning from Islamabad, we organized feedback sessions with the women artisans and shared the insights gained from the exhibition. We also explored strategies to expand their reach by participating in more international markets and establishing online platforms for direct sales. This laid the groundwork for a long-term vision of turning the Community Forums into a sustainable business network that could support hundreds of women, providing them with income security and a voice in the local economy.

Ultimately, our participation in the exhibition was not just about selling products; it was about creating opportunities, building bridges, and advocating for the potential of Afghan women in the global marketplace.

Shattered memories – A home turned into a place of fear

The trip concluded, I returned home with an indescribable excitement, an eagerness that came from the longing for home and family. During the journey, my mind was filled with countless thoughts, but as soon as I opened the door and entered the house, that excitement quickly turned into shock and disbelief.

At first glance, the house was strangely dishevelled. My heart raced, and at that moment, my daughter, with a distressed and worried expression, approached me. She anxiously said, "Mother, I have to tell you...the house was attacked."

The shock of this news was so overwhelming that I couldn't grasp all the details right away. My daughter explained that while we were away, local thieves had broken into the house and ransacked everything. As I slowly walked toward the rooms to assess the damage, fear and anxiety took root inside me.

Family heirlooms, precious gifts passed down through generations, were gone. Of all the stolen items, the one that broke my heart the most was a bracelet with twenty-one diamond stones. This bracelet had been a valuable family heirloom gifted to me during my wedding ceremony. It was more than just expensive jewellery – it was a symbol of love, memories, and family ties.

During our years of migration and fleeing from insecurity and war, I had carefully safeguarded these precious items. They were the only things that reminded me of my once secure and joyful past, something I no longer had in my life. But now, they had been taken by heartless thieves, and it felt like more than just material items were stolen. It was as if a part of my being, a piece of my family's history, had been lost.

This theft wasn't just a robbery; it felt like they had taken a piece of my soul. Something that could never be replaced at any cost. These valuable objects weren't just materially significant – they were spiritually important to me. The bracelet with its diamond stones wasn't just a piece of jewellery; it was a reminder of everything that mattered in my life, now lost in the hands of a heartless stranger. The home that once symbolized peace and security had turned into a place of fear and vulnerability. A space that no longer provided the sense of calm it once did.

This terrible incident revealed just how crucial security is in our lives. If someone had been in our home at the time, beyond the material loss, their lives could have been in danger. That's why we decided to send our son and daughter to Pakistan, where they could live in a safer, more stable environment with their uncle.

This decision meant that my husband and I would be left alone in Mazar-e-Sharif. This experience showed that in today's world, ensuring the security and peace of one's family is essential, and in facing dangers and threats, tough decisions have to be made. In this bitter chapter of life, more tough decisions would be necessary, bringing with them endless pain and suffering. After months of seeming peace and happiness in Mazar-e-Sharif, now the Taliban's invasion brought a new colour to the sky of the city – a colour of war.

Women in crisis – A tale of fear and hope

After a few months, the security situation in Mazar-e-Sharif rapidly deteriorated. The sudden Taliban attack sparked a war between Abdul Rashid Dostum's forces and the Taliban. We lived far from the city centre, and the situation became more critical with each passing day; it was as if the world around us was collapsing.

After the Taliban's retreat, the city seemed calm, but this peace wasn't for everyone. Anti-Taliban forces were searching for Taliban members, and rogue armed groups were involved in slander and theft. One day, a group of armed thieves attacked our home, demanding that my husband hand over his weapon – an excuse to rob us. My husband, who had no weapon, replied, "I don't have one. You can search wherever you like."

Without our children, my husband and I, being alone, were living with another family, our relatives, in a shared house. This family included a woman, her husband, and their child – displaced from Kabul – who stayed with us during those crisis-filled days.

At that moment, all of us were utterly terrified. Our home was engulfed in tension and fear, with every footstep and every word causing our hearts to tremble. Lacking the ability to defend ourselves against these armed individuals, we were overwhelmed with a deep sense of helplessness and vulnerability. The fear that the thieves might torture us or even threaten our lives had pushed us into a state of panic and intense anxiety.

With every passing moment, our dread and concern grew. The armed thieves, with their terrifying faces and threatening behaviour, searched every corner of the house while we sat in a corner, waiting for this horrific nightmare to end. At any moment, they could have escalated the violence and harmed us in the worst possible way.

This overwhelming fear and stress left us unable to think clearly or make decisions. Our lives were left to fate and the armed thieves, who could change everything in an instant. Each footstep and movement they made brought waves of stress and terror to our hearts.

After the armed men were sure there was no weapon, they left our home, but they took several valuable items with them. As we breathed heavily and trembled with fear, we realized that this horror might repeat. We could encounter other groups that would put our lives at risk. The anxiety of facing such circumstances again turned into an unending nightmare for us. This experience not only taught us bitter lessons about insecurity and vulnerability but also showed how, in times of crisis, humans can be pushed to their limits, gripped by fear and worry.

That same day, with only a few essential items, we sought refuge at a relative's house in the city centre and stayed there for fifteen days. The city remained in a state of war, and we were forced to decide to leave Mazar-e-Sharif. We never returned to our simple nest. This decision, despite all the hardships, revealed a painful truth about the struggles of life – a truth that shows how we must face such challenges with courage and strength.

Recalling these bitter and sweet memories is difficult, but I hope that this experience will be valuable for those who read it, and especially for young people who wish to learn from the history and experiences of a mother, a woman, and a sister. May they understand how a woman, as a nest-builder, carries heavy burdens to create a stable home for future generations. I hope this story, even if it makes just one person reflect, will be worthwhile.

Journey towards an unknown destiny

The unknown path of migration to Pakistan was the latest in our life experience. Those fifteen days were filled with new emotions and excitement at every moment. Ultimately, upon reaching our final destination and reuniting with family, these fifteen days became a permanent memory. What remained was not only memories of beautiful landscapes and historical attractions but also the many emotions and thrills we experienced during this journey, a time when the Taliban had taken control of Kabul during their first reign.

Once again, migration embraced us, but this time with a heavier burden than ever. Endless highways from one city to another witnessed the pain of separation and the warm embrace of farewell emotions. This time, with hearts more broken than before, we decided to leave our second home in Mazar-e-Sharif and move toward Pakistan, heading into an unknown destiny.

Our search for vehicles felt like a race against time. Along with a four-member family – a mother, her two young daughters, and her brother – we had to pass through dangerous and insecure cities, places where the shadow of Taliban dominance stretched from Afghanistan to the Pakistani border. This journey was filled with challenges and dangers, but despite all the hardships, we moved forward with hope for a better life.

Each point of this journey brought the novelty and excitement of a new challenge. Our encounters with local people and life in the cities and villages each told us a new story. In this journey, nothing was constant or stable, which filled our hearts with both fear and excitement.

Every day, as we crossed borders and the weather changed, our emotions trembled like an earthquake, swaying between hope and despair. But through all the hardships, a sense of resilience and strength always accompanied us. We were here, on a path full of adventure and unknown roads.

Amidst all these circumstances, migration felt fresh and unending for us. This journey not only separated us from home and family but also led us to a new and unfamiliar world. Leaving home and starting a new life for the third time, along with all these dangers and disappointments, was a significant challenge. But this challenge allowed us to prove to ourselves and others that we had the strength to advance along an unknown path of destiny.

The road wasn't easy. We set off again by taxi from Jabal Saraj District of Kapisa Province to cross through Kohistan District, passing through Nijrab and Tagab districts. It was early morning, still dark, and before dawn prayers, we had begun our taxi ride.

While crossing Kohistan District, we faced a terrifying and dangerous incident. A car ahead of us had been stopped by two armed men who violently robbed them of their belongings. When the passengers signalled for our taxi to stop, I was terrified, thinking they intended to harm us. But in reality, they had been victims of an armed robbery. Had we arrived moments earlier, we could have faced the same fate. The sight was horrifying – a narrow, rough, dusty road surrounded by trees and bushes, with danger lurking at every moment. The shadows cast by the trees only heightened our fear. Despite this, we had no choice but to continue our journey with hope and excitement. The taxi struggled along the rough dirt road, challenging the driver. Suddenly, a slip jolted our nerves. Fear remained etched on our faces as the taxi swerved off the road, its wheels stuck in uneven dirt, unable to move. The sudden event left us anxious and despondent, surrounded by the oppressive darkness of the road. It seemed no one would come to our aid, and we were alone, hopeless but for faith in God. Fortunately, the car eventually moved, freed from its trap.

At dawn, as the sun slowly began to rise, a magical atmosphere took over. Each ray of light brought the promise of a new day. With every deep breath, everything around us transformed into a stunning harmony. The sun's beams gradually covered the earth, turning everything into colour and light, and the leaves, quivering gently, seemed to sing the song of the morning.

After passing through the mountainous districts of Kapisa Province, our taxi journey ended. It was 8 a.m., and we needed to hire another vehicle to continue. However, the situation had changed. No cars were allowed to pass through Tagab and Nijrab districts. We were informed that travellers would have to proceed on foot, an announcement that unsettled us. We got out of the taxi and headed toward a steep dirt hill we needed to cross. We began walking, struggling alongside other families with little luggage. Exhausted, we reached the top of the hill just as the weather turned dark and rainy. The sudden downpour added to our unforeseen hardships. Everyone, carrying their few belongings, trudged through the rain, guided by the harshness of nature and unexpected surprises.

In the darkness of dawn, under immense hardship, we moved as fast as possible through the fields. Our hearts raced, constantly on alert, fearing the smallest danger. In this dark and merciless land, as we were passing through Taliban-controlled territory, we reached a wide but shallow river. Crossing it seemed difficult for the women and children, and hours of walking had exhausted everyone. The local Taliban had only one minibus available, allocated to the women and children, while the men had to walk. On the other side of the river, where the bridge had been destroyed by war, we waited for the men in cold and insecure conditions. But thankfully, we were spared from any life-threatening dangers.

The night was dark as we left our stop behind. After a tough trek, we reached Surobi, one of the districts of Kabul located between Jalalabad city and Kabul, and we spent the night there. The rough, dirt road still stretched ahead toward our destination. The exhaustion from the long walk was evident on our faces. We stayed in a simple tea house. In Afghanistan, tea houses – locally known as 'qahwa khana' or coffee houses – are very popular and common. People gather in these tea houses to drink tea, enjoy light snacks, and engage in conversations. Tea houses usually have a warm and friendly atmosphere and serve as a place for people to relax, share news, and meet friends and acquaintances.

In addition to tea, some tea houses also serve traditional Afghan snacks like Bolani, samosa, kebabs, Chainaki and even local sweets. Green tea and black tea are among the most popular drinks. These places are culturally significant and play an important role in preserving social relationships and facilitating cultural exchange. However, the tea house where we spent the night also had a small lodging area at the back, which could accommodate a minimum of three to five people. Despite this, around thirty of us ended up spending the night there. The conditions were not very hygienic, and the overall situation was far from ideal. Men's and women's rooms were separated, but both were sparsely furnished with thin rugs. The women and children, around 30 of us, sat together in a cramped room, where it was difficult to lie down or sleep, but we managed to get through the night despite the challenges.

This small tea house no longer had the comforting atmosphere of the past; signs of war were visible in every corner. The walls, once filled with laughter and conversations of travellers, were now marred by cracks and scars from distant explosions. A heavy ambiance prevailed, evoking a sense of loss. Each flicker of the dim light and the oppressive silence of the night whispered untold stories of hardships and survival. This place, once warm and tranquil, now held only memories of better days gone by. The next morning, we took a minibus toward Jalalabad city. Passing through Jalalabad had its difficulties too. At every step, Taliban checkpoints inspected passengers, asking questions about where we came from and where we were going. They paid special attention to men without beards and women without veils, often causing discomfort for travellers.

Our journey continued toward Pakistan, and we ended the night in Peshawar. This journey, filled with excitement and danger, marked our resilience and determination to survive. In Peshawar, we searched for a place to rest. After much effort, we found a relatively safe place under an unfamiliar roof, though our hearts were still filled with worry about the uncertain future. After only twenty days in Peshawar, I travelled back to Kabul. With the experience I had gained in establishing Community Forums in Mazar-e-Sharif, I hoped to assist women under Taliban control in Kabul. Driven by a deep sense of responsibility toward serving the community and empowering women, I saw this as a vital task. I would focus on providing job opportunities for women so they could become active and effective members of society, contributing to reducing poverty and improving the economic conditions of their families; boosting women's confidence and expanding educational and employment opportunities for them. These efforts would not only help reduce gender inequalities but also improve social and economic conditions, with the hope of witnessing impactful societal progress in the future.

Returning to Kabul, under Taliban rule and to my birthplace, filled my heart with mixed emotions. This decision not only reflected my commitment and responsibility to serving women and their families but also highlighted my deep connection to various aspects of life in my homeland, Afghanistan.

Chapter 7
Living and working under the Taliban

Establishing women's community forums

On the evening of Friday, September 27, 1996, Kabul had fallen under the control of the Taliban. This event marked a turning point in Afghanistan's history, ushering in a new era of instability and severe restrictions, particularly for women. After living in Mazar-e-Sharif for five years, I returned to Kabul – the city that had once been my home, full of sweet memories and familiar corners. However, now, Kabul seemed nothing more than a distant memory of the past. With the Taliban's takeover, profound changes had occurred in the city's face and atmosphere, changes that were almost indescribable.

My return to Kabul was not just a return to my home; it was about standing in solidarity with the people of my country, especially women. I decided to stand by them and seek ways to improve their social, cultural, and economic conditions.

With financial and technical support from UN-Habitat, Community Forums for women began operating in Kabul and gradually expanded to other regions of the country. One of the most significant and exciting missions during that period was the establishment of these centres, which began in the darkness of those times under complex and difficult conditions. Despite numerous concerns and doubts, we had to proceed with caution and precision, as every step we took was dependent on security and an uncertain future. Yet, these challenges could not hinder us.

The first step toward the success of these projects was establishing communication with the people of Kabul. These connections allowed us to identify the real needs and capacities of the people, helping them find solutions to their challenges. Our focus was on raising awareness and providing social education – programs that offered us the opportunity to implement social and economic development projects even in the midst of such a challenging time.

Among the educational activities were vocational and economic skills training, entrepreneurship and small business management, and teaching skills such as sewing, knitting, agriculture, food processing and handicrafts. Educational courses on school subjects were organized in a house-to-house manner for girls who were not allowed to attend school at that time. This program was designed to enhance their knowledge and skills in difficult and limited conditions, providing educational opportunities for girls.

Additionally, promoting environmental protection, fostering teamwork and cooperation, and teaching life skills like problem-solving, effective communication, and decision-making, as well as voluntary activities, literacy education, leadership and management development, and boosting self-confidence and self-reliance, were also key objectives of these programs. These initiatives were designed to enhance professional skills and empower women economically so that they could play an active role in supporting the livelihoods of themselves and their families.

Many women, through launching small businesses, became independent entrepreneurs. They not only played significant roles in the economic sphere but also contributed meaningfully to social and cultural issues. These centres became spaces for collaboration and the exchange of experiences, strengthening local social and economic networks. Both women and men were able to network and assist one another's progress. Over time, these centres became symbols of resistance, determination, and change in Afghanistan's history, proving that even in the most difficult circumstances, change is possible through strong will, guiding the community toward improvement.

The National Solidarity Program of Afghanistan, which is now recognized as one of the most successful development programs, has its roots in these Community Forums. At a time when Kabul was submerged in silence and fear, these centres became a beacon of hope – places where women could not only acquire new skills but also rediscover their own strength. The launch of this project was not just a social endeavour but a cry in the night, filled with the fear of threats that could jeopardize our lives. Yet, despite these concerns, we continued to give our all to turn this dream into reality.

These centres shone like lights in the darkness and will forever remain in my heart as a lasting reminder of boundless determination and hope that never fades. The establishment of women's community forums in Kabul, for the first time during the harsh conditions of the first Taliban regime, symbolized support and service provision to women. These forums not only provided essential services to women but also strived, under pressure and threats, to create opportunities for women's active participation in social and economic processes, ultimately improving their lives.

Encountering threats for the greater good

Our office operations for organizing women's community forums in Kabul were conducted under the guise of emergency aid and healthcare services in the office of Mary McMaken. She was an American woman who had lived in Afghanistan for over thirtyyears, and, as a woman over 65 years old, she had been granted permission to operate under the Taliban's authority. Mrs. McMaken rented an apartment across from Zainab Cinema in Shahr-e-Naw, Kabul. A physiotherapist by profession, she had been involved in supporting Afghan women, especially in the fields of handicrafts, tailoring, and aiding impoverished women.

In coordination with the UN-Habitat headquarters in Islamabad, we rented a room in that apartment for our activities. There, we operated completely covertly to avoid drawing attention from the Directorate of Promotion of Virtue and Prevention of Vice. Meetings were held in this office to establish communication with women from various areas of Kabul who were involved in empowerment programmes at different Community Forums. In addition, administrative tasks, and preparation of activity reports for the headquarters were also carried out in this space.

On a regular day, while we were working in the office and chatting with our colleagues, we suddenly heard the harsh and commanding voices of men from outside. Our hearts pounded rapidly – they were the Taliban! We quickly realized that their presence was not without reason; they had learned that women were engaged in activities in this building that, in their view, were considered "forbidden." They had come for an interrogation. The office door was closed, but the heavy sound of their footsteps echoed in the hallway, holding our breaths captive.

Suddenly, a loud banging on the office door shattered the silence. One of the Taliban members shouted in a sharp and threatening tone: "You are an infidel! Your work is forbidden!" With hostility, he pointed toward the handmade dolls – crafted with designs inspired by traditional Afghan clothing – creations made by skilled women who worked hard to support their families by selling them. Some of the crafts were shaped like animals but the Taliban had already declared this art "un-Islamic."

Then, in the midst of the suffocating silence, the sound of these artworks being smashed filled the room. One by one, the dolls were broken, and in an instant, the efforts and hopes of those women were reduced to ashes. Fear and anxiety gripped everyone. Moments stretched endlessly, and only one question echoed in our minds: "Who will be next?" Moments later, the door to our office opened, and a group of armed Taliban members entered. Sitting inside the room and only wearing headscarves as a form of hijab, we stood up, nervous and trembling, out of deference and fear. One of them, who seemed to be in charge of the inspection, asked in a dry and serious tone, "What are you doing here?" As I was responsible for women's affairs in Kabul province, I quickly replied, "We provide services to widows, the poor, and the needy, and we are trying to create job opportunities for them through their homes. Women who are responsible for supporting their families." His gaze was cold and lifeless, but his questions continued.

Another member of the Taliban asked, "Have you completed your education?" I thought he was referring to school or university education, so I quickly responded, "Yes, we are educated." But he repeated the question and said, "No, I mean religious education. Have you received religious teachings?" I replied, "Yes, we have learned religious teachings from schools, mosques, and our families." It seemed that this answer was not enough for the Taliban, as they continued asking my colleagues more religious questions. After the inspection and questioning ended, the person who appeared to be the leader of the group told me, "Come to our office tomorrow and provide more details about your work." I replied, "But didn't you yourselves issue a rule prohibiting women from entering men's offices?" He answered, "It doesn't matter. Some women come to our office."

With that, they left our office, but a deep sense of anxiety took over me. I was overwhelmed with worrying thoughts about what might happen. Initially, I decided not to go to their office but the next day, I received a call at Mary's office. The only available phone was part of the old government network of the Ministry of Telecommunications, as mobile phones were not yet in use. One of the women in the office informed me that I had a call. When I answered, it was the same man – the leader of the group that had visited our office the day before. After a brief exchange of pleasantries, he asked, "Why didn't you come to the office of the Authorities for the Promotion of Virtue and Prevention of Vice yesterday?" I made an excuse, saying that I didn't know the exact time. He then instructed me to come to the office the next day at 10 a.m.

Reluctantly, I decided to go the following day with two other female colleagues. When we reached the entrance, I saw the same Taliban man who was in charge of the inspection standing in the yard, talking to several others. When he saw us, he gestured from a distance to enter a room beside the entrance, which seemed to be the security guard's room. We entered and sat down on two long benches placed against the walls. We were fully covered, even our hands and feet were hidden. After about ten minutes, the Taliban inspector entered the room. We greeted him, and he responded. I introduced myself and remained covered. He immediately said, "I only wanted you to come alone, but you brought two colleagues with you. You don't trust us." I replied, "It's not about trust; it's because we work together, and nothing in our activities is ambiguous." At that moment, I still didn't understand the main reason why they had called me to their office. He began asking personal questions about my husband, what his job was, and where he was at the time. I answered that my husband worked in private business and travelled between Afghanistan and Pakistan and was currently in Pakistan.

It seemed they assumed that women were unfamiliar with religious matters, which is why they wanted to give me books to teach religious subjects to women. I told them we are all Muslims, and it is our duty to learn about religious and spiritual matters. However, I refused to come again into the office of the Directorate of Promotion of Virtue and Prevention of Vice.I explained that my family would no longer allow me, and in addition, their own laws prohibit women from entering offices. I also added that without the need to be physically present in the office, I would try to teach the cultural, Islamic, and Afghan values that I had learned from my ancestors and family to others. The inspector then added that some religious publications would be sent to that office. It seemed he had no further response to my words and perhaps only intended to test me. In any case, whatever the reason, I could not fully understand the hidden and ambiguous aspects of the situation, and thus, our meeting with the representative of the authority of Promotion of Virtue and Prevention of Vice ended, and we left.

Afterward, to avoid identification and tracking by the Taliban, we decided to stop visiting the apartment altogether. Nevertheless, the Taliban sealed the apartment and brought all public activities there to an end. This decision forced us to reassess and adjust our strategies to align with the new circumstances. In an environment filled with uncertainty and restrictions, flexibility and adaptation became essential. We strived to preserve our core objectives and find a new path to continue our activities – one that would both comply with the imposed conditions and uphold our mission of serving the community, especially women and needy families.

This story is a one of strength and resilience – a testament to the courage of Afghan women who, despite threats and fears, continue to stand strong and work toward a better future.

A desperate escape to safety

My sudden return journey to Pakistan began on a dark evening when the lights along the roads gradually went out. At home, amidst the silence of the night, a sound was heard, and two women activists from the seventh district women's Community Forum arrived. They informed me that armed Taliban men were searching for me. The locals had said that no one called Mahbooba was there, but the Taliban were still looking for more information. This was just the beginning of the story, and the women felt that these threats would soon become a reality.

With fear and despair imprinted on my hands, I decided that same night to seek refuge somewhere. I decided to go to Pakistan via Jalalabad, not knowing how long I would stay there. Early that morning, while the sky was still dark, I began my journey with my family members. The darkness of the night and the sound of our footsteps in the empty streets heightened our anxiety and fear with each passing moment.

The journey to Pakistan began mysteriously, but the closer we got to Jalalabad, the more our fear and worries intensified. We took various routes to avoid being spotted by the Taliban. It felt as if each step we took brought us closer to the brink of death.

It was only a month later that I set out on my return to Kabul once more. Leaving Pakistan was a decision of transformation and courage that guided me back to Kabul. Despite the difficult experiences, numerous threats, and various challenges, including security issues, I decided to return to help the brave women and people in my homeland who needed support and guidance in Kabul but needed to change my strategies.

Many women from different parts of Kabul joined me. They had the will and courage to make changes in their society too. Through collaboration with them, I realized that the most crucial need was creating equal opportunities for women to enter the workforce and become independent. But how could I bring about these changes?

I decided to share my ideas and perspectives with them secretly, with courage and confidence. Each of these women could build their own success stories. In fact, the women I worked with were symbols of power and ability, not only for themselves but also for other women. They united, shared their thoughts and dreams, and encouraged each other under cover of the burqa.

Women behind the burqa

My story

During the early years of the Taliban's rule, when their strict laws completely cast a shadow over the lives of the people, one of the most enforced regulations was the mandatory wearing of the burqa for women. At that time, there was no choice; every woman and young girl was compelled to wear the burqa, and no form of protest against this decree was accepted. Just like many other women, I too, as a woman, had no option but to comply. However, it didn't take long for me to become painfully aware of the difficulties and struggles that came with this obligation.

One of the first problems I faced was the difficulty in breathing beneath the burqa. Especially during the hot summer days, the scorching, humid air would weigh down on me, and a feeling of suffocation would take over my entire being. I constantly felt like breathing had become a struggle. On the streets, in alleyways, everywhere I went, I searched for a place where I could lift my burqa slightly and allow fresh air into my lungs. But in public gatherings or crowded spaces, I was never able to do so. In those moments, the sense of suffocation would engulf me, and there was no escape from it.

Another issue was the physical and health consequences of wearing the burqa. The skin on my face was under constant pressure, and the continuous sweating led to pimples and skin infections. My face was always red and inflamed, and I faced new breakouts every day. This condition not only became bothersome in terms of appearance, but the physical pain associated with it also turned into a nightmare. The burqa caused my body to be constantly subjected to heat and sweat. I felt as if I was drowning in a sea of heat and humidity with every passing moment. My skin became highly sensitive and damaged, and I never found relief. Especially during the summer days, each step I took felt heavier than the last.

Perhaps one of the greatest challenges, however, was the visual limitations and the serious dangers that the burqa posed. My vision was severely restricted under the burqa, and I was never able to see my surroundings clearly or fully. This issue became especially dangerous when crossing busy streets and crowded areas. Once, while crossing the street, I suddenly collided with a bicycle and fell hard to the ground. My head struck the pavement, and at the same moment, a car sped by just inches away from me. I could feel the intense pain in my legs, and a wave of despair and helplessness flooded over me. If I hadn't moved aside just in time, the accident could have been catastrophic.

It was around this time that I first experienced wearing prescription glasses for close vision. This experience, unexpectedly, became both eye-opening and painful for me. I realized that my eyes, under the pressure of the burqa, could no longer focus clearly. The glasses I was wearing acted like a window into a new world that I had been kept away from. On one hand, they helped me see the world more clearly, but on the other, this experience reminded me of just how deeply I was submerged in confinement and restriction. Every glance, every movement seemed to take me into a world separate from others, a world where freedom seemed as distant as a dream.

Wearing the burqa was not just a matter of clothing but a violation of women's individual rights and freedoms, stripping us of job opportunities. The restrictions in movement, in social interactions, and in business turned us into silent, powerless beings.

In such conditions, women were severely subjected to discrimination and denied opportunities, with their abilities and potential being taken away from them.

Living under the burqa was a daily battle. A battle against shallow breaths and endless pain, with health issues and serious limitations on choice and freedom. But despite all these challenges, we stood firm. The hope for a better future, for a life of freedom without constraints, continued to burn brightly in our hearts.

Meanwhile, during those early days, each morning was carefully and meticulously planned, with decisions made about which area and home each of us would go to. Our lives were filled with various goals and missions; from attending family gatherings to helping women in need, each day was designed in such a way that we, in the face of the pressures and constraints, would carry out our duties and keep the courage to resist alive in our hearts. The objectives we sought were not only to survive the exhausting days but also to preserve our hope and feminine identity.

We had multiple goals, ranging from participating in meetings and social councils to organizing training courses and visiting small and large projects that women had started in their homes to achieve self-sufficiency and support their families. However, every step we took was accompanied by fear and caution. We left our homes completely hidden beneath garments that not only concealed our bodies but also buried our identities and freedom beneath them. The oppressive regime loomed over us like a heavy shadow, and with each passing day, the pressure became more suffocating.

One day, like any other, I put on my chadari (burqa) and stepped out of the house cautiously. I passed through a narrow alley and approached the main road. My home was behind Zainab Cinema in Shahr-e-Naw, Kabul. As I prepared to cross the street, the small mesh opening in the burqa's face covering restricted my vision. I could only see vague shadows, but I had no choice but to keep moving forward. Every step I took was filled with anxiety – not because of the road itself, but because of the reality that had imprisoned women.

Suddenly, the burqa wrapped around my legs. I lost my balance and fell hard to the ground. The impact was so strong that a sharp pain shot through my legs, and my knees were badly injured. I remained there for a moment, pain coursing through my entire body, but what hurt me the most was the overwhelming sense of helplessness – not just because I had fallen, but because of a world that had forced me to hide beneath such clothing, a world that stole a piece of my freedom every single day.

But I got up. Like always, I got up and kept going. Because that was the only choice I had: to keep moving forward, to resist, and to stand against everything that sought to erase us in darkness. Struggling to get up, I realized that no one dared to ask if I needed help. I was a woman, and speaking to unrelated women was forbidden. This bitter experience reflected the harsh, dehumanizing conditions the Taliban had imposed on us. Yet, despite it all, we continued to resist with courage and determination.

No women happened to pass by in that moment either. Overwhelmed by despair, I found myself crying. No one offered sympathy or even asked how I was doing. I recalled the days when, as students or teachers at the university, we had walked past each other with respect and solidarity. Back then, if anything happened, our fellow citizens were ready to help one another.

With a heavy heart, I thought to myself, "How did we get here?" The same streets we had proudly and confidently walked just years earlier had now turned into places of cruelty and indifference. These unanswered questions lingered in my mind as I continued down the road, still holding onto the hope that maybe someone would muster the courage to help me. But no – on that day, I returned home without any help. There was no means of communication available to check on each other's well-being, as the civil war had destroyed all the city's infrastructure.

Sara's Story

Sara was a woman who once taught at Kabul University. Her eyes were always full of hope and dreams. In her classrooms, she worked tirelessly to introduce her students to knowledge and critical thinking. But one day, a time came when the Taliban took power in Afghanistan, and women's lives changed. Sara, who had always taught with pride and freedom at the university, was suddenly forced to hide in the dark world of the Taliban's restrictions.

With the rise of the Taliban, universities were closed, and women were no longer allowed to continue their education. Sara was also forced to stay at home. One day, as Sara was getting ready to leave the house, she heard her father's voice from behind the door: "A decree has come; you must wear the burqa." Sara stood still and looked down with a heavy heart. The burqa! Something she never imagined she would have to wear. With sorrow, feeling that she had lost her happy and free world, she put on the burqa.

Sara's bright, hopeful eyes, which had always seen the vast world of knowledge, were now enclosed behind a heavy covering. The burqa did not only cover her body; it imprisoned her soul in a cage. With every step she took, it felt like she was moving closer to darkness and invisibility. Though she wanted to walk into the outside world with pride and freedom, the burqa created a solid wall between her and the world.

In this difficult situation, Sara did not give up. Under the burqa, she secretly collaborated with other women to change the circumstances and improve the status of Afghan women. She communicated with other women through underground networks. These efforts were like a flame in the heart of the night, a flame that could have gone out at any moment, but Sara never stopped trying to support women.

A story of skilled hands and hopeful hearts

In the heart of Kabul, District One, women with skilled hands and hopeful hearts were engaged in quilt making and knitting jackets. These projects not only taught new skills to women but also enabled tens of thousands of them to benefit directly or indirectly from their production, filling their daily lives with determination and hope. It gave them the opportunity to use their abilities and earn an income for their families. This project was also a humanitarian initiative.

At the end of each period, the products made were distributed for free to impoverished families so that during the harsh winters and heavy snowfall, warmth from the hands and hearts of these kind women could reach their homes. This project was a symbol of solidarity, effort, and hope that brought life to the heart of Kabul.

Every morning, women's community forums across the city of Kabul began their activities simultaneously, filling with motivated and brave women. Women from around the city would come to these forums, not only to participate in long-term activities but also to engage in short-term programs and receive their raw materials and wages, which were part of short-term emergency relief projects. These forums acted as a station for launching new dreams. With their artistic hands, women would take the threads and begin sewing quilts and knitting jackets. The variety of colours and patterns, reflecting the diverse lives of these women, hidden under the shadow of the city's difficult history, added a special beauty to their work.

This project not only served as a bridge to improve the livelihoods of these women but also played a significant social role. The economy, revitalized by this project, had a significant impact on their lives. But more than anything, this project supported women who, with their innocent hands, were healing the wounds of war.

Behind these quilts and jackets lay stories of hard times, heartbreaks, and hopes for rebuilding lives. These products were delivered to impoverished families and helped reduce social and economic disparities.

The fabrics created with the tears and smiles of the women of Kabul were not only a moment of joy but sent waves of kindness and hope to the hearts of everyone there. The goods produced reached various cultures of the community, each holding special value for a particular life story.

This project was not only a symbol but also a beautiful plan for creating endless human connection and interaction. Just like water offered to the thirsty, this project was a lifeline for innocent, defenceless people affected by unwanted internal wars.

A flame of courage and solidarity

The day was cold and dusty, with the sun casting a dim light through the thick haze of dust that filled the air. A sharp breeze, laden with the scent of the plains, swept through the streets, carrying with it the quiet hum of waiting. In the District One Women's Community Forum, a group of women – around 40 – stood together, their faces etched with anticipation. They had worked tirelessly on short-term emergency relief projects, sewing and knitting colourful quilts and sweaters, each stitch a testament to their determination and skill. Now, as the moment to receive their wages drew near, they could only wait – for the wages they had earned with patience, precision, and the hope of something better.

At that moment, my two colleagues and I were suddenly summoned from District Seven to District One. Our goal was to oversee the process of distributing wages to the women. It had been reported to the Taliban that three women had arrived by taxi – targeting me and my two colleagues – claiming that men were also present in the centre, which was not true. While we were sitting in a large room, the sound of armed men in the hallway suddenly reached our ears. The surprise and fear had not yet left our faces when four armed men entered the room. In a rush, we all covered our heads and faces with the scarves we had.

The armed men hastily asked, "Where are the men? Why have you gathered here?" They in-quired about the leader of this group of women. With confidence, I stood up and replied, "I am responsible for this program. This is a support initiative for women, by women. No men are present here." My colleagues, brave and dedicated women, each explained their situation and emphasized our shared goal. With hearts filled with both fear and hope, we tried to show that these women had gathered solely to provide for their needy families. However, our response was met with violence and threats.

The armed men, in a commanding tone, said, "We should not see you here again. We will search everywhere, and if we find a man, you will face severe consequences." This threat struck our hearts like a heavy blow, yet in my colleagues' eyes, a flame of courage still burned. In that dark moment, more than anything, I felt a deep sense of peace in my conscience and an unshakable belief in the principles we upheld for women's rights. It compelled us to stand firm against violence.

As long as the armed men remained, fear cast its shadow over us. This experience vividly ex-posed the weaknesses and limitations that women had to endure. That day was not just about earning a wage; it confronted us even more deeply with the challenges and inequalities of life.

Planting the seeds of reason and logic

In the meeting with Taliban officials, we put forth a great deal of effort and courage to secure permission for women to work in these Community Forums through dialogue and reasoning. The main goal was to present logical, principled, and peaceful arguments to explain the importance of women's presence in the workplace for the society and economy of Afghanistan and to demonstrate that the role of women in society cannot be overlooked. We also emphasized that we, as women, work with women, so we asked them to allow it. We stressed that allowing women to work in forums would not only strengthen the economy and national growth but also enhance the economic stability of families.

Ultimately, the meeting with Taliban officials was an opportunity to convey, through reasoning and logic, the need for a change in attitudes toward women's rights and to find a way to improve the situation of women in Afghanistan.

In 1997, during the first period of Taliban rule, the Authority of Labour and Social Affairs was operated at the level of a General Directorate. In order to coordinate work with women, we tried to inform the relevant Taliban officials and prevent any issues that could hinder the progress of the projects. One of my male colleagues arranged a meeting with the head of the General Directorate of Labor and Social Affairs, and I went to that office.

As I approached the entrance of the building, the air around me felt heavy with anticipation. I was met by the stern gaze of the guards, their eyes assessing my every move as they directed me to a newly renovated room. This room, tucked away beside the gate, had a certain coldness to it, almost as if it held secrets that it was reluctant to reveal. It wasn't just the sterile walls and the sense of confinement in the air – it was the history embedded within those walls that spoke volumes.

The courtyard outside was adorned with trees, their branches swaying gently in the wind, almost as though they were speaking to one another. These trees, once a symbol of hope and strength, seemed to whisper of a time when women had once played an active and powerful role within the Women's Association. But now, as I looked around, that presence had been wiped away. The room, with its polished floors and sleek furniture, seemed to scream of an era where women's voices had been muffled, their contributions erased. It had become a place dominated entirely by men, and there was no trace of the energy and vibrancy that once belonged to the women who had fought for their rights. No sign of their struggle remained. The transition from a women's association to a male-dominated domain was not just physical – it was symbolic, a painful reminder of how easily progress could be reversed.

As I sat in that room, waiting for what seemed like an eternity, a sense of frustration slowly began to build up within me. Each passing minute felt heavier than the last. The walls, though newly renovated, felt suffocating, and the space seemed to shrink with every breath I took. My thoughts raced as I wondered about the purpose of this meeting. Was I here to simply observe the indifference of the powers that be? Was my presence here merely to serve as a token gesture, a hollow attempt to appease some unknown expectation?

After an hour, the wait was finally over. The door opened, and the man responsible for the meeting entered. He was a middle-aged man with an expressionless face and a slow gait, as if he were carrying the heavy burden of the world on his shoulders. He cast a brief, indifferent glance at me, as if I had disrupted his daily affairs. He announced that the meeting time had arrived and gestured for me to follow him.

As we walked through the hallways, my mind was occupied with predicting what would happen next. Where was I going? What was the purpose of all this? I walked in silence through the twisting corridors, thinking that the sound of my footsteps echoed in the space, while in reality, my shoes were silent. Eventually, we reached another part of the building. We entered a courtyard where the silence was unsettling. The atmosphere was tense, as if the courtyard itself was holding its breath. In the centre stood a solitary man. He was dressed in white, immaculate and well-groomed. He did not receive me in his office for a meeting; instead, he met me in the courtyard. Perhaps accepting the presence of a woman in his office was considered a disgrace to him.

As I approached, he turned slightly, as if reluctant to speak directly to a woman. After I greeted him, he responded coldly. His demeanour made it clear that his reply was nothing more than a dry, obligatory formality. His body language conveyed indifference. At that moment, I realized – this meeting was not a meeting of two equals.

My heartbeat quickened, but I composed myself to speak. I knew that the road ahead would not be easy, but I was here for a purpose, for a mission. This was not a time for doubt. Taking a deep breath, I began to speak. My voice was firm yet full of emotion. I spoke about the necessity of women's employment in the country, emphasizing that this was not just about their rights but about survival. I reminded him of the women who had lost their husbands, brothers, or sons in the civil war – of women now trapped in poverty; their lives reduced to a struggle for survival. Many of them were widows, some disabled, and all vulnerable. They needed jobs. They needed stability. They needed a purpose in life.

These women were victims of unwanted wars in Afghanistan. Their stories were filled with pain, yet they were also full of hope and determination. They had endured unimaginable hardships, yet they still had something to offer. It was essential that the government and the leaders in this institution understood this truth. Women's employment programs were not just about creating jobs – they were about restoring their dignity, their autonomy, and their ability to provide for themselves and their families. It was about giving them the opportunity to rebuild their lives from the ruins of a war that had shattered everything they knew.

As I spoke, I felt the weight of his gaze on me. But it was not a gaze of empathy. It was not a gaze of understanding. It was a gaze of indifference, as if he were simply waiting for me to finish so he could dismiss me and return to his "more important" matters. His posture remained stiff and formal, as if he was deliberately trying to ignore the impact of my words and distance himself from the depth of emotion they carried.

Despite his cold demeanour, I continued. I spoke about the importance of implementing sup-port programs for these women – programs that would provide them with the tools needed to rebuild their lives and communities. I spoke of the necessity of creating opportunities, not just for the women who had lost everything, but for future generations. I reminded him that the stability of the country depended on empowering women. If action was not taken now, the cycle of poverty, violence, and inequality that had inflicted deep wounds on the nation would persist.

When I finished speaking, a long silence filled the air. The space we stood in seemed to swallow my words, as if they had already been forgotten. The man in white gave me a fleeting glance, his expression blank and unreadable. Then he spoke, but his words were devoid of any real promise or commitment. He said he would keep me informed, that he would consider what I had said. But deep in my heart, I knew these words were nothing more than a polite deflection – a way to end the conversation without addressing the real issue.

That day, I walked out of that building with a deep sense of disappointment, but not surprise. I knew what kind of environment I was stepping into. I knew the road would be difficult, that resistance would be fierce, that the fight for women's rights would be a long battle. Yet, as I walked away from that meeting, I could not help but feel that at least I had done my duty. I had spoken the truth, regardless of how uncomfortable it was for those men. I had conveyed the voices of the women who needed support, and in doing so, I did not allow their voices to be silenced.

I had come to that meeting for a purpose – to defend the forgotten women – and I left with renewed determination. Their struggle did not end with my meeting. It continued, and I stood beside them, every step of the way.

In the end, I realized that this fight was far from over. It was not just about one meeting or one conversation – it was about years of effort, relentless pressure for change, and the unwavering demand for equality. And although the response I received that day was, at best, cold and indifferent, I knew that the seeds of change had been planted. They might not grow immediately, but they would grow. That, I was certain of.

Empowerment from within

Based on information I heard from a public source. I later learned that during the early days of the Taliban's rule, a woman had actually held meetings at the Taliban's General Directorate of Labour and Social Affairs to address women's issues, in a room that had previously hosted activities and services for women, managed by women under the name of the Women's Institute. The fact that this institute existed in a male-dominated space filled me with hope when I heard the news, and I decided to visit that office at the earliest opportunity.

Without prior notice, I went to the gate and asked the armed guard to allow me to enter. I hesitated for a moment, but my resolve was firm. Gathering my courage, I asked him to let me in. The guard looked at me for a moment and then, with a gesture, directed me inside. While twisting myself nervously, a lingering sense of worry still surged within me. After undergoing the necessary checks, I was directed to a building that seemed both powerful and mysterious. Its structure, like the environment inside, demanded submission, yet it also promised influence and change. As I walked through the dimly lit corridors, my heart pounded fiercely in my chest, but I was determined to ensure my voice would be heard that day. I knew I had something to say.

The room I entered was silent, perhaps too silent. The walls were bare, and the air felt heavy and tense. In one corner of the room, a woman sat alone, fully focused on her papers and pen. All the women in the room were sitting, in turn each voicing their concerns one by one. However, there was something about a particular woman that set her apart from the others. She sat in a corner of the room, separated from the rest, her posture rigid and proud, as if she saw herself as superior to the others.

A feeling of discomfort overtook me as I waited for my turn. Every woman who spoke before me seemed to be struggling to express her issue. Amidst the growing layers of futility, I moved closer to facing this woman in the corner of the room, who paid no attention to our concerns.

When my turn came, she glanced briefly at me, but the look was not warm. On the contrary, her gaze was sharp and concerned. Without any interest, and without introducing herself, she asked me, "What is your problem?" With the patience I could muster, I began to defend women's rights. I spoke from the heart, for I knew that the issue I was raising was not just a personal one. It was the struggle of many women, like me, who had faced challenges imposed upon them solely because of their gender.

As I spoke, I soon realized that she was not paying attention at all. She stared at her papers, gently writing with her pen, as though she were just passing time, not truly listening to my words. There was no comment, no reaction, no sign of understanding. She simply said, "I have noted the issues. I will inform you." And with that, my words hung in the air, unanswered. A wave of disappointment surged within me, but I pushed it aside. I had no hope, but just the fact that I had spoken was valuable to me. That day, I left the room, feeling invisible, my voice swallowed up by an indifferent system.

Days, weeks, and months passed, yet I never heard back from that unknown woman. I couldn't believe it. Despite speaking with all my heart, I received no response. I didn't feel any change.

Years later, when political changes began in Afghanistan, and the Taliban's rule came to an end, that woman – who had ignored my plea at the time – was now in a position of authority. How had she reached such a position? In a time when other women faced tough and limiting circumstances, how had she found herself in such a role.

As things settled and the country began to rebuild, the truth became clear. The woman I had met that day had become one of the key figures. She was no longer indifferent. She had risen to a position where she could be a decision-maker regarding the fate of many. This is one of those hidden necessities of history for women, where outward indifference is a necessity to obscure the underlying intention of building empowerment from within.

Empowerment under cover

Our temporary office operated under strict confidentiality in the Maternity and Gynaecology Hospital located on Kabul's Shopping Road, also known as Froshgha. This office was established as a central hub for regular administrative activities and to facilitate communication with all community forums in the neighbourhoods of Kabul. In return, we provided financial and technical support to the Maternity and Gynaecology Hospital for Women.

This office was not only a place for administrative work but also recognized as a centre of hope and effort for the women in our community. Every day, brave and hardworking women came here to collaborate and strive for a better future for themselves and their families. Despite the existing challenges and threats, everyone continued their activities with strong determination and hope for better days ahead.

One of our greatest achievements was empowering women and providing them with educational and job opportunities. By holding workshops and various training courses, women were able to acquire new skills and increase their economic independence. With each passing day, we witnessed the growth and progress of women who continued their efforts with motivation and hope for a brighter future.

However, after a few months, I was suddenly informed that we must leave the hospital immediately and without delay. The reason for this urgent action was that the Taliban had become aware that three women were conducting various activities for women in the neighbourhoods of Kabul and were likely coming to arrest us.

This news hit me like a sudden shock, but we could not easily surrender. With hearts filled with fear and hope, we quickly exited the hospital. Every moment could have brought the Taliban to our door, but we were determined to continue our struggle.

As I hurried out of the hospital, my eyes suddenly fell on one of my close friends, Zarafat, who was sitting with patients from around the hospital, basking in the sunlight. Although I had known her for years and wanted to go to her, I couldn't stop. With a heavy heart and tearful eyes, I passed by Zarafat unnoticed. Later, I heard that my kind, brave friend had passed away due to illness, spending her last moments comforting others. That moment when I could not approach my dear friend and tell her how much she meant to me will always stay in my mind. This ideal and the memory of Zarafat remained in my heart and served as motivation to continue fighting for the rights and well-being of women.

After leaving the hospital, we established a new office in a more secure and hidden location. During those difficult times, the support and collaboration among us women grew stronger than ever. We continued our work, expanded our educational and supportive programs, and strived relentlessly for the women of Afghanistan.

Now, looking back and reflecting on the path we have taken, we see that our efforts have not been in vain, and we have managed to create positive and lasting changes in society. This journey is far from over, and although many challenges lie ahead, with unity and solidarity, we can step towards a better future for all women in Afghanistan.

The final days of the Taliban Regime

In the history of every nation, there are moments that change its fate and create narratives that remain in the memories of people forever, becoming part of history. The final days of the Taliban regime in Afghanistan were one such period. Those days, alongside political and military crises, pushed the people of Afghanistan to the brink of ultimate pain and suffering. Security across the country, especially in Kabul, became an increasingly growing threat.

Although Afghans have always been resilient in the face of challenges, no one could deny that security in Kabul, especially after the martyrdom of Ahmad Shah Massoud, was under serious threat. The situation was growing more and more critical with each passing day. Some people tried to escape the country and sought refuge in neighbouring countries. Pakistan became the destination for many who, in fear and anxiety, tried to escape the atmosphere of insecurity and an uncertain future. In such conditions, anyone living in Kabul felt they had to seek refuge somewhere with less risk to save themselves and their families.

We were all trying to save our lives. Everyone headed toward a place they considered safer, whether inside the country or abroad. Some families migrated to other provinces, while others travelled illegally to Iran or Pakistan, even without passports. For many, these journeys were akin to fleeing from death. Nothing was more important than saving lives, and everyone was trying to test their chances of survival in this time of terror and insecurity.

In these circumstances, our family decided to go to Pakistan. We had our passports with us and knew that travel to Pakistan was possible for those with valid documents. However, at the last moment, when we reached the Torkham border of Pakistan, the border soldiers announced that due to security issues, even those with passports would not be allowed entry. In that moment, the faces of many people behind the border seemed sad and desperate. We, who had expected to cross the border and reach Pakistan easily, suddenly had to turn back toward Kabul.

Returning to Kabul meant going back to a city that was unpredictable and full of security threats. For us, this return was accompanied by feelings of despair and deep concern. We spent the night at a relative's house in Jalalabad city of Nangarhar province, and that night, our hearts never found peace from the endless worries and fears. The next morning, with hopes that the security situation in Kabul would improve, we decided to head back to Kabul. Even though we knew the conditions were still unstable, we rented a vehicle and set off once again.

The security situation in Kabul remained extremely worrying. Threats were heard from every direction. Unrest and internal conflicts were growing every day. Many parts of Kabul were under intense attacks, and no one could predict what would happen day to day. As a result, we had to take shelter for a while in the home of another relative in the Chahar Asiab district. This area of Kabul was relatively safer than other parts, and we lived there for about a week.

In the following days, nothing frightened us as much as the fact that we were still in danger. Eventually, we decided to attempt the mountainous route from Jalalabad to Pakistan. This decision meant embarking on a journey full of additional risks. The high mountains, narrow dirt roads, and nothing but threats to the lives of travellers turned the trip into a final insurmountable test. But for us, there was no other choice. We had to leave Kabul; we had to escape this situation by any means.

The journey to Pakistan under such circumstances was one filled with fear and anxiety, each moment accompanied by endless concerns. This journey was not just a physical struggle; it was an emotional life saving journey of a future that was at risk. At every step, the fear of instability and the terror of the unknown accompanied us, but we had no choice but to continue. This journey was a journey born of anxiety and despair – a journey we had to endure for survival and the hope of a better future.

A dangerous journey through the mountains

The journey did not begin with energy and enthusiasm, but rather with overriding fear of an uncertain fate. The paths ahead had no law other than the law of guns and power. Armed and irresponsible individuals charged money to transport people to Pakistan.

With a precise map, we first had to walk on foot through the mountains and then navigate the high dirt hills in unreliable Datsun vehicles. Each step we took became a new challenge, leading us around an unknown mountain.

Despite the difficulties and dangers, we successfully traversed the mountains. Those towering peaks, touching the clouds, stirred various emotions within us. There was no opportunity to rest; we had to keep moving without pause.

Excitement and fear coexisted within us simultaneously. As we approached the summit, the challenges grew more daunting. The journey to the peak was fraught with new challenges, from winding and dangerous paths to extreme climatic changes. Cold winds, seemingly coming from the very outer limits of the sky, accompanied us.

When we neared the final heights, the view from above was breathtaking. The world beneath us pulsed, and we felt small and insignificant against the larger universe. Within these fearsome mountains, ancient legends were etched into the air, and anyone who climbed their peaks would uncover a new world of secrets and unknown mysteries. On this journey, we faced new boundaries. But when we reached the summit and stood peacefully above the earth, everything felt valuable. This journey not only transported us to a remote place but also allowed us to connect more with ourselves and the world, learning the freshest life lessons with each step.

By the time we reached Pakistan, nothing had been simple. Our blood had dried on our hands. This difficult and frightening experience left eternal memories and, even in those hard moments, reminded us of deep human encounters and the terror of life.

The narrative of history that preceded our return to Kabul reflects such terror when after the attacks on the Twin Towers of the World Trade Centre in New York on September 11, 2001, the United States commenced its military operations in Afghanistan, named "Operation Enduring Freedom". Afghan forces, under the umbrella of a coalition led by the United States and the "Northern Alliance," captured major provinces one after another.

On November 13, the Taliban retreated from the capital Kabul and from Kandahar, their stronghold in the early days of their emergence, and with the coalition's airstrikes, the Taliban's rule came to an end. After the fall of the Taliban regime, Afghan leaders gathered at the Bonn Conference held in Germany in December 2001, where they appointed Hamid Karzai, who was later elected as president, to lead the interim government of Afghanistan and bring forth a new era.

Chapter 8
The beginning of a new era

Returning home

Our return to Afghanistan after a month during Hamid Karzai's rule was marked by regime changes. Crossing the Torkham border, I left behind a calm yet trembling city and, from the moment I set foot in Kabul, I experienced new stories. This time, my path was not through dusty valleys and chaotic mountains, but along busy roads that unfolded like beautiful tales of new life before me. The green fields and blue sky intertwined, igniting my motivation to return home. Entering the vibrant city of Kabul filled my heart with joy, and life, with all its youth and colours, welcomed me back.

The home to which I returned was not nestled among towering mountains but located in Shahr-e Naw, behind the Zainab Cinema. This house symbolized the transformations that had taken place in this land. Again, in this place where the melodies of life resounded, I settled and began anew.

This time, joy filled my heart, a joy in knowing that women were now allowed to participate in social, economic, political, and cultural activities without unnecessary restrictions. The burqa was no longer compulsory for women. They proudly wore outfits that fully protected their social identity, moving freely among the community.

During the rule of the Taliban, women were deprived of their basic rights and were not allowed to work officially or freely in any field. However, with the rise of Hamid Karzai's government, new doors opened for women, and opportunities for employment and social participation were made available to them.

As I looked back, I realised the depth of the changes. Seeing women confidently and calmly present in various fields and spaces filled my heart with joy. This change symbolised the beginning of a new era of significant transformations and unique opportunities for women in society.

We, the female employees of the United Nations Human Settlements Programme (UN Habitat), had taken a major step towards equality as part of these changes. In the workplace, men and women worked equally and cooperatively side by side. Women were no longer limited to household duties; they collaborated with men on various projects and played significant and impactful roles.

The courageous presence of women in these areas not only revealed their social identities but also created an inclusive and fair space for all members of society. These transformations clearly demonstrated the capabilities, skills, and pivotal roles of women in building a better future for society.

Women, like birds set free, could now express themselves in any field they chose. Their presence was prominent not only at home but also in offices and projects. This change marked a turning point in the history of society, demonstrating that women's identity and power could not remain in the shadows.

At the time a question formed in my mind: "In a society, how can one expect justice and equality to prevail without the active and determined presence of women?" This city, now filled with the vibrant and powerful presence of women, was moving toward a hopeful future full of new possibilities. Yet, despite this significant transformation, changes in the realm of power had not completely faced all challenges. Administrative structures had not been completely rebuilt, numerous challenges remained, including issues related to water systems, electricity, transportation, environmental health, medical services, trade, and the lack of sustainable strategies for utilizing natural resources to alleviate poverty and create employment. These challenges stemmed from various periods of changes in governance, as well as wars and internal conflicts, which had negatively impacted the basic necessities of the people and remained a reality.

The need for sustainable planning to utilize natural resources for poverty reduction and job creation required special attention. We had to seek solutions that positively impact the economy, local communities, and environmental preservation. Facing such challenges can lead to a dynamic and sustainable society through the equal effort and cooperation of both women and men. Although the path ahead was difficult, through unity and solidarity, we can overcome such obstacles and lay the groundwork for a brighter future for generations to come. Empowering women in all areas is the key to achieving this goal, and only through equal participation can we attain balanced development and social justice.

Idea for the establishment of the Afghanistan Women's Business Council

Women in Afghanistan have always faced a turbulent fate, experiencing more judgment, cruelty, and oppression than any other group. Despite this, the historical background of Afghan women is somewhat bright, and their activities are commendable. Women in Afghanistan have always been active in various fields, including scientific, cultural, literary, social, political, and economic realms.

The *covert revolution* of women during the first five years of Taliban rule (1996-2001) stands as one of the most challenging periods, marked by secretive activities aimed at transforming Afghan society. This era played a significant role in establishing and developing social development programs, particularly through the establishment of women's Community Forums, which later provided an opportunity to establish the Afghanistan Women's Business Council (AWBC) after the regime change. This council focused predominantly on women's economic empowerment.

During those five years, through secretive and risky activities, women laid foundations for a new era via social development programs that led to the establishment of the AWBC. The economic and social empowerment programs were pivotal in transforming communities and were implemented cohesively and precisely, especially targeting women's empowerment. Like flowers that bloom from the heart of the earth, bringing forth beautiful branches and leaves, these programs expanded retaining their careful attention to community needs.

Those who were trained in the community forums came together like *soldiers* with a clear mission. With their active participation and acquired knowledge in various fields such as education, small and medium enterprise development, vocational programs, literacy, handicrafts, and marketing, they played a significant role in enhancing women's capabilities in society.

Before the establishment of the AWBC, in November 2002, I had been invited by the Women Entrepreneurs Organization of India to attend an international conference on women entrepreneurs. This invitation came due to my experience as the founder of the first official women's business, the Khorasan Cooperative. The conference and exhibition in India provided a unique opportunity for sharing experiences, establishing new networks, and exchanging ideas for the development of women's businesses. As a representative of the Khorasan Cooperative, this trip was a great honour for me, as I met individuals active in the field of women's economic empowerment internationally and introduced our latest achievements in this area to others. This journey was not only an opportunity to promote women's businesses but also an effective strategy to enhance the role of women in international communities.

The India Conference and Exhibition was held for two weeks. During this time, women from various countries participated in numerous sessions, and I also attended as a panel member. Due to my experience and business background in Afghanistan, I had the honour of receiving an award symbolizing the resilience of women in self-sufficiency, which was presented to me on behalf of the women of Afghanistan.

Upon returning to Kabul, a special conference was launched. At this special conference, attended by experts, researchers, and activists in the field of women's rights, a new and transformative idea emerged regarding the need to support the economic empowerment of Afghan women. This idea, like a spark in the darkness of overwhelming challenges, shone brightly and quickly captured the minds and hearts of the attendees. The proposal to establish an organisation focused on strengthening the economic capacities of Afghan women emerged during the discussions and exchanges – an idea not only stressing the necessity of supporting women in this field, but also serving as a key to unlocking new opportunities and independence for them.

This idea swiftly moved from the realm of thought and theory into the practical sphere. Following this, in group meetings with active Afghan women, the proposal to establish the "Afghanistan Women's Business Council" was brought forward. As the coordinator and liaison for this process, I devoted all my energy to conducting regular surveys with women and establishing effective communication with governmental and non-governmental organisations active in the field of women's economic empowerment. These meetings were not only filled with empathy and solidarity but also fostered a remarkable atmosphere of brainstorming and unity, which sped up the process of shaping this innovative idea.

Drawing on my experience in cooperatives and the commitment I had to the economic empowerment of women, I devoted all my efforts to ensure the new organisation was quickly registered and established. After months of persistent work and challenges, we finally succeeded in officially founding this nascent centre through a collective determination and hard work.

A group of women gather for an awareness session led by Mahbooba, focused on starting small businesses using local resources to economically empower women, promote local production, and encourage their active participation in economic activities.

After the establishment of the council and my election as CEO, I dedicated myself fully to advancing the Council's goals and establishing its strong foundations. Initially, with proper financial management and the support of UNIFEM, the council was able to begin its initial activities effectively for two and a half years. Later, by creating a self-sustaining and independent structure, the council succeeded in establishing a wide network across Afghanistan.

With strong, professional leadership and a deep understanding of the needs of Afghan women, the council became a powerful and influential entity in the country. The council's focus on the importance of empowering women and providing self-sufficiency skills training led to significant achievements in the economic empowerment of Afghan women. These achievements not only helped women gain financial independence but also restored their dignity and self-confidence. Afghan women, now motivated by a renewed sense of purpose, took bold steps towards progress and change in their country. These successes not only improved the status of women but also sparked a wave of hope and movement towards a brighter future across Afghanistan.

Steps towards commitment and progress

In 2003, I, alongside a group of inspirational women, had taken a significant step towards improving the economic status of women in Afghanistan by establishing the Afghanistan Women's Business Council. My professional journey had begun in 1987 with collaboration in the Khorasan Cooperative, and since those early days, I have focused on developing women's business activities across Afghanistan. This journey reflects my strong determination to achieve social and economic goals for Afghan women, accompanied by a steadfast commitment to progress.

Over the years, we have led and implemented various programmes aimed at improving the economic conditions of Afghan women. These initiatives included organising training courses, business awareness and creating business networks that helped women enhance their economic power. This path was accompanied by numerous challenges, but with strong determination and commitment, we continued to pursue these goals, as we believed that the economic progress of Afghan women is crucial not only for themselves but for the prosperity of the entire Afghan society. With perseverance and resilience, we have continued our efforts for a brighter future for all Afghan women, working towards a country that progresses towards sustainable development and social justice.

In the history of every country, institutions and leaders who seek to elevate the social and economic status of a particular community have always faced numerous challenges. In Afghanistan, which has experienced many ups and downs throughout its history, the role of women in social and economic changes has become more prominent, especially in recent decades. In this context, I believe that commitment and progress are two terms that are vital not only for Afghan women but for the entire society and the country as a whole.

Commitment – the foundation of every progressive movement

At first glance, the word "commitment" may seem to mean merely a strong and enduring decision. However, when we look at its social and economic impacts on societies like Afghanistan, we see that this term carries a much heavier significance than it might initially appear. Commitment to changing the economic status of Afghan women means faith and confidence in the power of transformation and change. This commitment allows Afghan women to tap into their inner capacities and create job opportunities, earn income, and improve their standards of living.

The founder of any progressive movement in the field of women and economics in Afghanistan must first believe in change and then tackle it with perseverance and strong will. Commitment in this journey means facing challenges, ups and downs, and even temporary setbacks. The establishment of the Afghanistan Women's Business Council in 2003 by a group of pioneering women was a crucial step in strengthening the economic status of Afghan women. This action was not just a managerial or economic decision but represented the unwavering commitment this group of women had to changing their situation and that of their society.

However, commitment alone is not enough. Real and sustainable economic and social change and progress can only be achieved when this commitment is accompanied by a clear strategy, proper planning, and continuous effort.

Progress – the result of collective efforts

Progress in today's world is not just about achieving personal or group goals. Progress is a collective phenomenon that arises from interactions, collaborations, and shared experiences. On a national level, progress occurs when many women and men work towards improving each other's social and economic conditions. In Afghanistan, this progress in the economic sphere of women is not only about the growth of individual incomes but also about the enhancement of the community's economic power.

On my journey, numerous actions and programmes have been carried out over the years to empower Afghan women towards economic progress. For example, organising training courses in various professional and business fields for women has been one of these programmes. These courses prepared women both academically and practically, enabling them to start successful businesses and participate effectively in society.

The creation of business networks helped women connect with others, exchange experiences, and discover new job opportunities.

These business networks not only increase the economic power of women but also foster a sense of solidarity and mutual support among them. This, in turn, contributes to economic growth and progress on a national scale.

Challenges and obstacles on the journey to progress

On the path of progress and change, there are always numerous obstacles and challenges that can slow down or even halt the movement. These obstacles in Afghanistan, especially in relation to women, are manifold. Such challenges include cultural limitations, gender inequalities, the lack of suitable educational and employment infrastructure, and security issues.

In many parts of Afghanistan, especially in rural areas, women still face traditional and cultural views that prevent them from engaging in economic and social activities. However, none of these challenges can stop the determination and commitment of Afghan women to progress. Every challenge and obstacle becomes an opportunity for learning and growth. These women, with unwavering determination and unparalleled resilience, are always striving to change the circumstances and build a better future for themselves and their communities.

Ultimately, commitment and progress are the two key elements for creating a bright future for Afghan women and Afghan society as a whole. When these two principles are combined, they can become a driving force that can lead Afghanistan towards sustainable development and social justice.

Chapter 9
From historical participation to contemporary collaborations

The impact of women in Afghan society

Empowering women is one of the key elements of social and economic development in any country. In Afghanistan, the establishment of the Afghanistan Women's Business Council has been one of the most prominent achievements and effective steps in this regard. This council has provided a platform for women entrepreneurs to amplify their voices in economic and social spheres and secure their position within the country's structure.

Human history is a testament to the active and influential presence of women in various social, cultural, and economic fields. In many societies, even with social and cultural limitations, women have been able to play a central role in the development of their communities. In Afghanistan, despite widespread challenges, women have always been active in various economic and social domains. These women have not only played a significant role in advancing the country's economic and social development but have also taken remarkable steps toward creating positive changes in society through their impactful actions.

The Afghanistan Women's Business Council has given women the opportunity to strengthen their presence in society and achieve greater influence in various economic and social fields. Furthermore, this council has played a crucial role in areas such as networking, training, and enhancing women's managerial and business skills.

The past is full of examples of women who, with strong determination and following the pioneers of the business world, have brought about significant positive changes in their communities. One of the most notable examples of this was Hazrat BiBi Khadijah, who was recognized as a great businesswoman and entrepreneur in her time. The loyal wife and an effective partner of the Prophet Muhammed (S), offering unwavering support at every stage of his life., but she also actively engaged in economic and trade activities using her wealth and knowledge of business management. Today, inspired by such prominent figures, women have been able to play key roles in strengthening family systems and participating in social, cultural, and economic development. These inspiring histories prove that women can play a fundamental and decisive role in the transformation and progress of societies.

The Women's Leadership Forum Conference

To promote economic participation and strengthen women's leadership in entrepreneurship, one of the most significant and fundamental steps in this direction was the organization of the Women's Leadership Forum in 2004. This conference included group workshops across various economic sectors, providing women with the opportunity to engage in discussions within their specific fields of expertise. Participants analysed strengths, weaknesses, challenges, and potential solutions, aiming to identify effective strategies for overcoming obstacles and advancing women's roles in the economic sector.

In this conference, a group of women entrepreneurs, experts, government officials, and representatives of international organizations gathered to discuss key issues related to increasing women's participation in various economic sectors, fostering an entrepreneurial spirit among them, and expanding job opportunities for women. This event provided a valuable platform for Afghan women to showcase their abilities, achievements, and experiences in different business fields while openly addressing the challenges they face in entrepreneurial development.

One of the fundamental topics discussed in this conference was the importance of active female participation in Afghanistan's national economy. Particularly in a country that has endured years of war and crises and requires economic reconstruction and transformation, the role of women as an active workforce and entrepreneurs has become more critical than ever. The conference emphasized that without women's involvement in the country's economic development process, achieving economic and social prosperity would not be possible.

Mahbooba leading a workshop during the Women's Leadership Forum held in Kabul in 2004 to strengthen women's leadership and promote their economic participation.

Supporting women entrepreneurs was a central theme of this event. Many speakers highlight-ed the necessity of backing women's initiatives and projects across different business sectors and proposed various strategies to strengthen this domain. These suggestions included providing educational opportunities, improving access to financial resources, and establishing suitable platforms for networking among women entrepreneurs to facilitate the growth and development of their businesses.

Another significant topic discussed in the conference was enhancing women's leadership capacities in the business sector. Developing and improving leadership skills among Afghan women, particularly in the business world, was one of the event's key objectives. The conference aimed to prepare Afghan women for leadership roles in organizations and businesses and to equip them with the necessary expertise through specialized training sessions and workshops.

One of the notable achievements of this conference was the creation of an opportunity for Afghan women entrepreneurs to exchange experiences and knowledge. Additionally, the presence of representatives from international organizations helped strengthen Afghan women's position in global markets and created new opportunities for the expansion of women's businesses.

The challenges and obstacles that Afghan women face in their entrepreneurial journey were also specifically examined during the conference. These issues included limited access to financial resources, the absence of effective support networks, and a lack of specialized training in various business and financial fields. To address these concerns, the conference held specialized sessions to propose practical solutions while also sharing successful experiences from other countries in supporting women entrepreneurs. These experiences demonstrated that with adequate support and active participation, Afghan women could overcome challenges and achieve significant success in the business sector.

The active participation of Afghan women in the "Leadership through Coordination and Participation" conference at the national level also had a wide-reaching impact. This event significantly enhanced the image of Afghan women in the global business arena and sent the message to the international community that Afghan women are capable and talented and can play a key role in the reconstruction and economic development of Afghanistan.

Conferences became an effective platform for Afghan women that not only helped increase their self-confidence but also provided the necessary motivation to expand their business and entrepreneurial horizons both locally and globally. Ultimately, this movement strengthened the position of women in Afghanistan's business community and increased their participation in the country's economic development process. As a result, the first national conference was not only a major and influential event in the history of Afghan women but is also regarded as a turning point in empowering women economically and creating new opportunities for them. This conference continues to serve as a model for all emerging and developing movements, demonstrating how harnessing the potential of women across various sectors can contribute to sustainable and comprehensive development.

From small beginnings to active participation in the national economy

The history of Afghanistan testifies to the presence and participation of women in all economic sectors, particularly in agriculture and industry. Female farmers, despite facing numerous limitations in land ownership, have played a fundamental role in the country's agricultural economy. They form a vital part of the informal economy and have made significant contributions in this field. Moreover, traditional handicrafts such as carpet weaving, kilim weaving, embroidery, and jewellery making have long been domains of activity for Afghan women artisans. However, documenting their history and narratives has always been a challenge.

As mentioned previously, for the first time, in the mid-1990s (1370s in the solar Hijri calendar), a group of women, using their personal investments, founded the "Khorasan" cooperative. This cooperative, which operated in the production of various handicrafts, succeeded in officially registering the first commercial joint-stock cooperative in Afghanistan's history.

Subsequently, in 2002, I represented this cooperative by participating in an international conference of women entrepreneurs in India. Upon returning to Afghanistan, together with other like-minded women I initiated the process of establishing the Afghanistan Women's Business Council (AWBC). The council focused on mobilizing women in small businesses and empowering them economically.

In October 2003, AWBC was registered as an independent, non-political, non-profit, and non-governmental organization. Over time, this council grew and became a self-sustaining institution, providing diverse services to women entrepreneurs and assisting them in registering their enterprises under the Ministry of Commerce and Industry.

Over many years, the council has established more than 50 business associations in Kabul and other provinces. These associations operate in various sectors, including handicrafts, transportation, construction, education, food production and processing, tailoring, weaving, and the revival of pharmaceutical factories. Overall, these efforts have supported more than ten thousand female entrepreneurs.

AWBC has functioned not only as an independent entity but also as a bridge between women entrepreneurs and governmental and non-governmental institutions. The council has collabo-rated with social organizations in both urban and rural areas, striving to address the needs of businesswomen in all sectors.

One of AWBC's priorities has been to support rural and vulnerable women. By raising aware-ness, the council has encouraged women to obtain identity documents and participate in savings and loan groups. Additionally, through collaborations with service complexes and economic empowerment projects, the council has found that, despite many challenges, rural women have always been eager to establish businesses and engage in private commercial activities.

The council has undertaken extensive initiatives to strengthen women's role in commerce and create a suitable environment for them, including:

- *Facilitating women's participation in training courses and business events.*

- *Providing access to modern machinery.*

- *Establishing connections with financial institutions for loan acquisition.*

- *Allocating land in industrial parks for women entrepreneurs.*

- *Producing high-quality products with innovative designs.*

- *Offering short-term and long-term educational opportunities.*

- *Participating in international conferences, seminars, and exhibitions.*

- *Disseminating information through websites and media.*

- *Coordinating with companies and business associations.*

- *Supporting women in accessing investment opportunities.*

- *Increasing women's participation in the economy and strengthening their productive and commercial capacities.*

AWBC continues to strive to strengthen women's position in Afghanistan's economy, aiming to turn them into key players in the country's economic development. We believe that providing equal opportunities for women is the key to building a strong, independent, and prosperous Afghanistan. With the commitment and perseverance of its members, the council will continue its path toward sustainable development of women's empowerment in order to play a transformative role in the national economy.

Reflection on sustainable development impact

Sustainable development means improving the social, economic, and environmental quality of life both now and for future generations. This concept focuses on principles aimed at meeting the current needs of society without compromising future resources and capabilities.

The main goals of sustainable development include:

Preservation of Natural Resources: *Through responsible consumption and optimal management, sustainable development seeks to preserve natural resources for future generations.*

Enhancing Quality of Life: *This includes sustainably meeting basic needs, improving living standards, and enhancing health and education conditions.*

Economic Balance: *Sustainable development pays attention to the balance between the economy, society, and the environment to prevent disruptions and enhance equilibrium in social and economic development.*

Social Justice: *The goal of sustainable development is to ensure that all individuals benefit equally from opportunities and advantages of development.*

Support for Sustainable Industries: *Promoting industries and economic activities that cause minimal harm to the environment.*

Civic Participation: *Active participation and engagement of citizens in decision-making related to development are fundamental principles of sustainable development.*

Technological Development and Innovation: *Utilizing technology to improve social and economic performance while reducing negative environmental impacts.*

Addressing Climate Change: *To preserve ecological systems and biodiversity and to combat climate changes.*

Therefore, sustainable development is a broad framework that considers economic, social, and environmental dimensions to improve the quality of life both now and for future generations. This concept emphasizes the responsible use of natural resources, enhancing quality of life through health, education, and economic balance, and promoting social justice to ensure equal opportunities for all. By supporting sustainable industries, encouraging civic participation, and advancing technological innovations, sustainable development aims to create long-lasting positive impacts while addressing critical issues like climate change.

One key opportunity in achieving sustainable development lies in empowering women, particularly in sectors like business and agriculture. Organizations such as the Afghanistan Women's Business Council play a crucial role by bridging the gap between governmental and non-governmental institutions. By promoting women's active participation in business, these organizations are nurturing a new generation of capable women who can play a pivotal role in the economic and social development of their communities. This approach not only supports women's empowerment but also contributes to the broader goals of sustainable development through economic growth, social equity, and environmental sustainability.

Women of impact – pioneers of change

Through the ups and downs of recent decades, amidst hopes and challenges, the names of those who have shone as pioneers and influential leaders of the Afghanistan Women's Business Council (AWBC) have been etched in history. These individuals have not only witnessed Afghanistan's social and economic transformations but have also been among the architects of change and development in the field of women's trade.

Among these outstanding figures, Dr Nasima Masood, Kabira Ziafi, Nasima Payman, Hossai Andar, Zarghona Walizada, Humaira Shekiba Habiba Azimi have each played a crucial role in decision-making and advancing the council's goals with their unique qualities and lasting impact.

Dr Nasima Masood, relying on her academic knowledge and expertise, has laid the foundation of the council's decisions based on scientific reasoning and documented analysis. Kabira Ziafi, with a deep understanding of social issues and representation of marginalized groups, has always emphasized balance and justice in executive processes. Nasima Payman, possessing exceptional managerial skills and outstanding practical abilities, has infused a wave of dynamism and energy into the council's social movements.

Hossai Andar, with her insightful political and social analyses, has contributed to a better understanding of contemporary challenges and ways to overcome them. Zarghona Walizada, utilizing creativity and innovation, has constantly sought new solutions to improve citizens' living standards. Habiba Azimi, with a strong sense of responsibility and commitment to society, has built a solid foundation for a sustainable and shared future.

On this challenging yet honourable journey, figures such as Ramin Qari Zada, Said Zarif, Nabila Osmani, Humaira Shakiba, Rubina Asad, Mari Enayat and other executive committee members have played a key role in achieving the objectives of the Afghanistan Women's Business Council. With dedication, expertise, and solidarity, they have mapped out a path for women's growth and empowerment in trade, marking a turning point in the country's economic history.

Documenting these efforts and contributions not only highlights the role of women in Afghanistan's economic development but also serves as an inspiration for future generations. While it is impossible to detail all achievements and efforts in this brief text, it must be acknowledged that every individual and every decision, like a valuable piece of a grand puzzle, has played a role in the council's success.

We sincerely appreciate all those not here mentioned who have accompanied us on this difficult yet rewarding journey. Your commitment, wisdom, and tireless efforts have played a pivotal role not only in improving women's economic conditions but also in elevating their social status. The dedicated and purposeful services of the council's senior members have not only led to an improved standard of living for citizens but also set an example of coordination, solidarity, and collective effort in achieving social and economic goals. These achievements present a dynamic and hopeful picture of a brighter future for Afghan women, reflecting growth, trans-formation, and resilience on the path to women's empowerment in trade.

Zarghona Walizada

One of the most prominent, inspiring, and influential figures in this field: Zarghona Walizada, was a trailblazer of the Afghanistan Women's Business Council. With her unwavering commitment and unparalleled passion for elevating the status of women in business, she has secured a shining place within this institution. From the very beginning, she has actively participated in all Board of Directors' scheduled meetings, events and activities, playing a key role with enthusiasm and energy.

With a higher education in administration and commerce from Kabul, Zarghona was nominated by the council for training courses in the United States and Italy to further enhance her skills and knowledge. Through her dedication and motivation, she has become a recognized figure not only within the council but also at the national and international levels.

One of her outstanding achievements is the establishment of *Tak Taz,* a Transport and transit company that has successfully gained independent membership in the Afghanistan Chamber of Commerce & Industry. As the first female investor in the fields of freight forwarding and transport in Afghanistan, Zarghona has courageously overcome all challenges and has uniquely provided national and international transportation services for commercial and transit goods. Under her inspiring leadership, this company has become one of the most successful entities in the field of transit and freight forwarding.

In addition to her role on the board of the Afghanistan Women's Business Council and the Afghanistan Women's Chamber of Commerce & Industry, she also serves as the chairperson of the board of the Afghanistan Freight Forwarders and Transit Union (AFCO). Through her strong leadership and foresight, these organizations have played a significant role in strengthening the position of women in business.

Zarghona is recognized not only within Afghanistan but also internationally as a symbol of the tireless efforts of Afghan women entrepreneurs. In 2018, she was named the Best Woman Entrepreneur of Afghanistan by the South Asian Association for Regional Cooperation (SAARC) and received the "Recognition for Good Business" award.

In addition to her business successes, she has been repeatedly recognized for her humanitarian services. Numerous awards from cultural and international organizations in Europe testify to her exceptional commitment to serving the people of Afghanistan. Zarghona Walizada is a symbol of strength, resilience, and inspiration for all Afghan women. She has demonstrated that with faith in one's abilities and relentless effort, one can break boundaries and reach the peaks of success.

Dr Nasima Masood

Dr Nasima Masood, a prominent figure in our country, is an exceptional and distinguished woman in today's world. She is a loving mother, a supportive wife, and a caring sister. With advanced

From left to right: Dr. Nasima Masoud, Kubra Zaifi, and Mahbooba Waizi. This picture was taken in Dushanbe, the capital of Tajikistan, during their participation in a conference and exhibition showcasing Afghan women entrepreneurs.

education in dentistry and expertise in the field, Nasima provides excellent medical services and is deeply dedicated to their care.

In addition to her professional responsibilities, she dedicates significant time and energy to raising her children and plays a prominent role in her home and family. As a board member of the Afghanistan Women Entrepreneurs Council, she actively participates in all decision-making, meetings, consultations, and related activities, representing women at national and international conferences and exhibitions.

Nasima is another prominent and influential figure on the board of the Afghanistan Women's Business Council. Since the establishment of the council in 2003, she has been an active and encouraging member, quickly gaining the trust of others through her sincerity, warmth, honesty, and integrity. Elected as a board member by a majority vote, she has played a key role in advancing the council's objectives with her creative and constructive insights. She not only actively participated in important council meetings and decision-making processes but also emerged as a powerful and influential voice for Afghan women entrepreneurs at national and international forums. Her tireless efforts have guided the council toward remarkable achievements and the realization of Afghan women's dreams.

Women in Afghanistan face challenging conditions, and those who have been forced to migrate also grapple with their own unique challenges – Dr Nasima Masood is one such woman – currently living in Vancouver, Canada and despite being far from her homeland, she has never lost hope or determination. Always expressing her concerns through phone calls and other communications, she strives to assist her fellow women with her valuable advice and experiences.

With a big heart and strong will, Nasima strives to amplify the voices of Afghan women wherever she goes. She generously shares her experiences and insights to help other women navigate difficult paths. Every call and message she delivers carries a message of love and hope for improving the situation of Afghan women.

Her presence and activities, even from the most distant places, exemplify a strength and motivation that nothing can deter. Through her unwavering efforts and persistent endeavours, she reminds others that nothing can break the human spirit and will. She is a symbol of hope and resilience that motivates Afghan women and other migrants to never give up on their efforts and to fight for a better future.

Kubra Zaifi

Born in the historic city of Herat, the pleasant atmosphere of her hometown always inspired Kubra Zaifi to be optimistic. Her story is that of a woman with an iron will and a heart full of courage who, shines like a beacon of hope.

Kubra is recognized as a pioneer in supporting women entrepreneurs in Herat. She completed her primary and secondary education in local schools and then pursued higher education at Kabul University. After graduating from the Faculty of Pharmacy at Kabul University, during the difficult times of the Taliban regime, she worked as a pharmacist at Herat Hospital, providing specialized and scientific training to women and girls when access to education was severely limited.

In 1999, Kubra joined the United Nations Human Settlements Programme (UN-Habitat) and undertook various roles, especially in social development programs and the establishment of Women Community Forums in Herat. Despite numerous challenges, she never wavered in her support for women and continued her efforts despite adversity.

She was also a prominent member of the board of the Afghanistan Women's Business Council and, with the establishment of the Afghan Women Business Union in 2005, created a remarkable movement in her beautiful home city of Herat. Through her tireless efforts, she strengthened support for women and identified those who lacked access to professional skills. With the backing of the AWBC, she provided diverse training programs for small business startups and marketing, opening many new doors for women. She became the voice of women entrepreneurs at national and international forums and conferences.

Kubra's life extends beyond the borders of Afghanistan. She migrated to Canada, where she continued her activities. As a consultant in various organizations, including AWO and CCVT, she supported women and war victims. With her exceptional spirit and outstanding abilities, she is not only a loving and empowered mother but also a remarkable role model for Afghan women in their struggle for rights and freedoms. With every step she takes, she shows women that every dream can become a reality with determination and perseverance.

Suraya Parlika

An inspiration for women's advancement Suraya Parlika, as the president of the All-Afghanistan Women's Union, played a pivotal role in advancing the economic rights of women. This union, as the first collective entity, became a member of the Afghanistan Women's Business Council. Through this achievement, she was able to implement significant activities for the union's members and create the necessary conditions for women's economic growth. Her unparalleled commitment and leadership helped establish a more prominent and impactful presence for Afghan women in the commercial and economic sectors. Born in 1944 in the village of Kamari, in the Bagrami district of Kabul, in 1962, she graduated from Zarghuna High School, and in 1966, she earned her bachelor's

Suraya Parlika, with Mahbooba

degree from the Faculty of Economics at Kabul University. She then continued her studies in Ukraine and in 1973, she obtained a master's degree in international economics. Her tireless efforts, honesty, and selflessness in serving the community reflected her deep belief in the empowerment of women and her hope for positive change in Afghanistan. Her works and achievements still remain in the hearts of many Afghan women and continue to be a source of inspiration for future generations.

Suraya not only encouraged women to participate in business activities but was also influential in the field of vocational and technical education. She played a key role in improving the social and economic status of women in Afghanistan and contributed to fundamental changes in society. As a pioneer in women's rights and an economic activist, she also served as the head of the ARCS Afghanistan's Red Crescent Society from 1986–1992, where her effective humanitarian leadership led to the advancement of social and humanitarian services in the country.

She also played a significant role in the drafting of the new Afghan constitution, which clearly reflected her tireless efforts to improve the rights and status of women in society. She will remain an eternal symbol of resistance, commitment, and the pursuit of justice and equality in the hearts and minds of the people of Afghanistan.

Suraya also made valuable contributions to the community as a member of the AWBC and later as the chairwoman of the Afghanistan Women's Business Federation of Women Entrepreneurs. Her election as chairwoman was the result of a competitive vote and the unwavering trust of the majority, and she fully committed herself to paving the way for the growth and development of Afghan women.

Her passing in 2019 (1398) left a wave of deep sorrow and grief in Afghanistan and beyond. She had devoted her entire life to women's rights and social advancement, brought about significant changes in society with her passionate leadership. Her loss was not only a great pain for human rights and women's activists but also created a deep void in the social and economic fields of Afghanistan. Nevertheless, Suraya Parlika's legacy remains inspirational. Her relentless efforts for justice and equality will remain in the hearts and minds of many, especially for the generations who continue to uphold her dreams. May her soul rest in peace, and her memory be eternal!

A journey of hope and solidarity – *the Canadian and Afghan Women Entrepreneurs in the Pursuit of Business Development and International Engagement Conference*

In 2003, with the start of an energetic period, the Afghanistan Women's Business Council made history and opened a new chapter for Afghan women. Formed by a pioneering group of women, the council became a symbol of hope for women in Afghanistan. Far away, a team, composed of Canadian businesswomen – Barbara Mowat, Anu Agarwal, Emma Quinn, and Jennifer McMillan, were among the first delegation members to travel to Afghanistan, aiming to share their global business programs with Afghan women. They visited Afghanistan as the AWBC was being established. This trip was not only a historic event but also demonstrated women's determination to enter the business realm, highlighting the value of solidarity and cooperation between Afghan women and those from other countries.

At the conference and exhibition held in honour of the Canadian delegation, Afghan women not only showcased their products but also demonstrated that Afghanistan is capable of progress and holds hope for the abilities of its community. They shone like a light in the darkness of this field. Their presence not only illuminated the path for Afghan women but also instilled in them confidence and hope to achieve their goals.

In 2003, as the Afghanistan Women's Business Council was being established, a group of Canadian businesswomen – Barbara Mowat, Anu Agarwal, Faye Back Emma Quinn, and Jennifer McMillan – travelled to Afghanistan. This photo shows these pioneering delegates during their historic visit, which aimed to support and collaborate with Afghan women in advancing their role in business.

This journey was not just a business experience but a significant lesson in the lives and businesses of young Afghan women. The delegation served as an inspirational source for emerging women entrepreneurs in Afghanistan, encouraging them to take impactful steps toward developing their own businesses with confidence and innovative ideas.

As the CEO of the council, I proudly and enthusiastically hosted the Canadian delegation, taking another step toward the development and progress of Afghan women, showcasing that women can lead and manage with talent and determination in any field.

In one of her online posts, Barbara noted that she felt anxious before entering Afghanistan, wondering whether Afghan women were ready to embrace changes in product development and trade. However, that anxiety dissipated as a hundred women from every province participated, and a singular beautiful Afghan woman took the stage, microphone in hand, declaring: "With one hand, we rock the cradle, and with the other, we will shake the world."

Women welcomed the Canadian delegation with appreciation and joy. At the conference, the delegation members eagerly and sincerely shared their insights with Afghan women, as contracts and memorandums were signed and sealed a plenty.

Barbara Mowat

Barbara is the President and Founder of GroYourBiz Ltd. and Impact Communications Ltd., specializing in consulting, management training, and international business development. With over 35 years of experience, she has supported thousands of businesses worldwide and launched initiatives like the Uniquely Programs, benefiting 12,000 Canadian entrepreneurs. A recognized leader in the development of SMEs across Canada, Asia, the USA, and other regions, Barbara has made significant contributions to fostering entrepreneurship. Through GroYourBiz™, she offers peer advisory boards for women entrepreneurs, promoting leadership and growth. Barbara also serves on various boards and committees dedicated to business development and has been honoured with numerous awards for her commitment to advancing women's economic empowerment.

Barbara writes on her organization's website: "Our world has become dramatically smaller, and whether this smallness adds to the charm of life is an interesting question. From Afghanistan to Ottawa to London (UK)! Despite geographical distances and diverse lives, friendships and connections remain, making this reality of life more fascinating."

My first meeting with Barbara in 2003 occurred during her trip to Afghanistan. In 2011, I had the opportunity to reconnect with Barbara at a conference in Ottawa, where we discussed various challenges and future plans, making the most of our reunion. Our next interaction came in 2019 through social media while I was in London, leading to further discussions over Zoom. We have continued to stay in touch through social media, with the shared aspiration of organizing another exhibition in Canada, highlighting the participation of Afghan women.

As I was preparing for a trip to Canada, I realized how, as time passes and wherever we are, friendships endure. Our friendship story is like a strong, enduring thread that, whenever intertwined, certainly adds colour and fragrance to a fascinating life.

An inspiring journey – contributing to the empowerment of Afghan Women

In today's challenging world, personal and professional experiences can serve as guiding lights for others. This is the story of Khaloud Al-Khalidi, who travelled to Afghanistan in 2003 as a program manager to help improve the status of women in the business sector. The aim of this program was to provide a suitable framework for the development of Afghan women's entrepreneurship and their empowerment.

Ms. Khalidi was a knowledgeable, patient, and kind woman. She sincerely shared all her knowledge and expertise with Afghan women. She showed deep respect for the culture and customs of the people of Afghanistan and adhered to them carefully. She presented the educational content using an excellent and impactful method, which created a warm and engaging classroom environment.

The educational materials prepared by her were so effective that, even today, they continue to be circulated and utilized in various workshops. An important point to note is that translations of these materials were also made available to Afghan women, ensuring that everyone could benefit from them. Her journey emphasizes the strength and determination of Afghan women to create change and achieve sustainable progress and self-sufficiency.

Khaloud Al-Khalidy with a group of women entrepreneurs at the end of training in 2005 at the headquarters of the Afghan Women's Business Council in Kabul — the collective efforts of women taking on economic roles and expanding the network of female entrepreneurs in the country.

A path to entrepreneurship and economic development – collaborating with the International Labour Organization (ILO)

Afghanistan, a land of legends and challenges, embarked on a two-year program from 2003 to 2005, supported by Italy, aimed at sowing the seeds of entrepreneurship among its women. This project, led by Khaloud Al- Khalidi and launched in collaboration with the International Labour Organization (ILO) International Training Centre, sought to build institutional and technical capacities for empowering women in the field of entrepreneurship.

The role of active national partners, especially the Afghanistan Women's Business Council, was crucial in this endeavour. These collaborations provided Afghan women with the opportunity not only to acquire new skills but also to gain greater self-confidence and self-reliance. The empowerment of women in Afghanistan not only transformed their lives but also significantly contributed to the country's economic and social development.

This program, as a symbol of collective will and sustained efforts, paved the way for Afghan women to build a brighter and more hopeful future by relying on their talents and capabilities. The changes brought about by this empowerment have not only impacted the individual lives of women but have also ignited a spark for progress and prosperity within society. Women's empowerment is the key to sustainable development in Afghanistan and holds the potential to shape a brighter future for the country.

Entrepreneurship development and handicraft for women in Afghanistan project

With Italy's support, this two-year project was launched to promote women's entrepreneurship development through micro and small enterprises, as well as to enhance the quality of women's handicraft production in Afghanistan. The project was initiated by the Bellisario Foundation and implemented jointly with the International Training Centre of the ILO.

The objectives of the project were three-fold:

- To build institutional capacity for women entrepreneurship development (WED) in Afghanistan by providing training for a large number of women trainers, advisors as well as women entrepreneurs through local women focused organizations.

- To develop the technical capacity of Afghan trainers to provide training and technical assistance to women entrepreneurs in Afghanistan in the field of enterprise development and handicraft quality improvement.

- To create linkages between women entrepreneurs in Afghanistan and potential markets and sources of technical expertise in Italy.

The WED project strategy aimed to guarantee the sustainability and continuity of the project through upscaling project outcomes learned from three phases:

1. Training needs analysis: assessment and identification of training needs and priorities

2. Implementation of main training activities
3. Coaching and follow up technical assistance in Afghanistan

More than 250 Afghan female participants benefited from the project training activities (whether in Turin, Italy or in Afghanistan) through which they were able to acquire knowledge and skills in enterprise as well as improving their handicraft production quality.

A training capacity of Afghan female trainers and advisors was developed and established within national partner institutions who began implementing training activities for promoting WED in different parts of Afghanistan. Until September 2005 Afghanistan Women's Business Council project partnerships trained more than 600 women in business awareness in different regions, while Care International trained more than 120 women by September 2005.

Tailor-made training materials for promoting WED in Afghanistan was developed and translated into local languages. These materials are widely used by project trainers and national partner organizations as well as other international and local development organizations.

The project "Entrepreneurship Development & Handicraft for Women in Afghanistan" aimed to foster women's entrepreneurship and improve the quality of Afghan handicrafts with Italy's support. It focused on training women entrepreneurs, creating linkages to international markets, and building the capacity of local trainers – benefiting hundreds of women and establishing a network for ongoing women entrepreneurship development across Afghanistan.

Empowering Afghan women entrepreneurs – the Artemis Project

One of the other programs aimed at enhancing the capacity of Afghan women entrepreneurs that provided significant services was the Artemis Project. This program was designed with careful consideration, and a key component of it for implementing educational initiatives was the mentorship program. In this program, a mentor would work closely with a woman entrepreneur, guiding and supporting her in practically implementing her business endeavours.

I had the privilege of working with two esteemed mentors: Peggy, who sadly passed away later due to cancer. Peggy's experience was in New York city at the Fashion Institute of Technology in advanced concepts in fashion design, processes, marketing, production.

The second was Meredith Peabody, with whom I worked in 2005 as part of the Artemis Entrepreneurial Program at Thunderbird University in Glendale, Arizona, US, focusing on financial management. Meredith deeply admired the resilience, strength, and unwavering determination of Afghanistan women in the face of challenges. To her, these women were not only entrepreneurs but also pioneers, breaking barriers and paving the way for future generations. She often spoke of their courage and commitment, which left a profound impression on her and motivated her to support them wholeheartedly.

A Memoir of the Artemis Project – Meredith Peabody

'Upon meeting the Artemis cohort for the first time, I was instantly captivated by the energy and determination radiating from the Afghan women entrepreneurs gathered for the program. Here were women so far from home, each a beacon of resilience, courage, and ambition, ready to embark on a transformative journey. The program, designed to equip them with essential business skills, aimed to foster sustainable enterprises that could thrive in Afghanistan's challenging landscape.

As we began to share our stories, I was struck by the unbelievable narratives of these women – stories forged under oppression. Many spoke of their lives under Taliban rule, where basic freedoms were stripped away and dreams felt impossible. I listened, mesmerized and heartbroken, as they recounted their experiences of resilience in the face of adversity. They spoke of the constant fear that dictated their lives, detailing how they could not leave their homes without a male escort or had to take different routes each day just to avoid detection. The most heart-breaking aspect of their stories was the lack of access to education. Many recounted how girls were forbidden to attend school, their dreams of learning extinguished by oppressive mandates.

From the outset, the atmosphere of the Artemis program was charged with hope and possibility. I recall my first day, mingling with women from various provinces, each with a unique story and a vision for their future. They had left behind their homes, traveling to the United States for two intensive weeks of learning, dreaming of the impact they could make upon *returning. This was more than a training program; it was a lifeline, a chance to rewrite their narratives.*

The curriculum was both rigorous and inspiring. Under the guidance of Thunderbird, The Global School of International Management's esteemed faculty, the women delved into business fundamentals – finance, marketing, and strategic planning. But what benefitted them the most was the personal coaching sessions. Each woman worked closely with a mentor to refine her business plan, transforming abstract ideas into concrete strategies. I was privileged to be one of the mentors and witness moments of clarity and empowerment as they articulated their aspirations, confronting doubts with newfound confidence.

Yet, the journey didn't end with the two-week program. The real work began as they returned to Afghanistan, where the complexities of establishing and expanding their businesses awaited. I felt a profound sense of responsibility as a mentor, knowing that my support would play a crucial role in their ongoing success. Regular check-ins and coaching sessions became vital lifelines, helping them navigate the challenges they faced in their unique contexts.

Reflecting on this experience, I realized that Project Artemis was not just about business training; it was about igniting a movement. It was about cultivating a network of empowered women who were committed to changing the narrative for future generations. The program's impact reached far beyond individual businesses; it fostered a culture of entrepreneurship that resonated throughout Afghanistan.

In the end, the journey through Project Artemis taught me as much as it taught the Afghan women. Their bravery, resilience, and unwavering commitment to their dreams served as a reminder that with the right support, no dream is too ambitious, and no barrier is insurmountable. Together, we tried to build a brighter future – one entrepreneurial spirit at a time.

Meredith Peabody September 26, 2024

The Regional Women's Economic Network (RWEN)

Other integral network and conferencing collaborations between Afghanistan, Pakistan, and Tajikistan in promoting women's entrepreneurship were equally significant. Members of this RWEN initiative include the Afghanistan Women's Business (AWBC), the Association of Women Entrepreneurs of Pakistan (AWESOME), and the National Association of Women of Tajikistan (NABWAT). The objectives of these collaborations include strengthening women's entrepreneurship through the following measures:

Expanding Entrepreneurial Opportunities: Creating and developing new opportunities to strengthen the capacities of female entrepreneurs in Afghanistan, Pakistan, and Tajikistan.

Facilitating Networking and Exhibitions: Organizing exhibitions and networking opportunities between AWBC, AWESOME, and NABWAT to better understand market demands and establish effective communications.

Promoting Learning and Experience Sharing: Strengthening the process of mutual learning and peer support between participating associations to enhance collaborations and leverage each other's experiences.

These collaborations aimed successfully to create a dynamic and effective entrepreneurial ecosystem and improve the business conditions and economic activities for women in these three countries.

Women entrepreneurs from Afghanistan, Pakistan, and Tajikistan in the Dubai exhibitions – a regional collaboration to empower women economically and expand business, learning, and networking opportunities.

Reflections on the role of conferences and exhibitions

Conferences within the Regional Women's Economic Network (RWEN) have played a significant role in promoting women's entrepreneurship. Conferences generally provide opportunities for exchanging experiences and ideas in the field of women's economic development, strengthening regional cooperation, and facilitating networking among organizations and stakeholders in this field. Through these events, the values of empowering and supporting Afghan women have been promoted and have had a positive impact on their economic capacities. Conferences and regional exhibitions are of great importance for women entrepreneurs and can have wide-reaching positive effects. Some of these benefits include:

Networking and Connections: *These events provide excellent opportunities for connecting with other entrepreneurs, investors, and advisors. Connections can lead to collaborations, partnerships, and even finding valuable mentors.*

Access to Resources and Support: *Exhibitions and conferences often serve as platforms to introduce products and services to a broader audience. This helps women entrepreneurs connect with customers, investors, and media, and find new resources.*

Training and Learning: *Many of these events include workshops, lectures, and educational panels that help women entrepreneurs acquire new skills and knowledge. These trainings can be effective in improving business strategies and addressing various challenges.*

Inspiration and Motivation: *Attending such events can be motivating and inspiring for women entrepreneurs, especially when they hear success stories and experiences from others. This can boost their confidence and enthusiasm for their endeavours.*

Exposure to New Markets: *Exhibitions allow entrepreneurs to showcase their products and services and reach new customers. This can help expand market reach and increase sales.*

Receiving Feedback and Constructive Criticism: *These events provide a great opportunity to receive feedback from experts and potential customers. This feedback can help improve the quality of products and services.*

Creating Investment Opportunities: *Many exhibitions and conferences feature sections for presenting projects and attracting investors. This can create opportunities to secure funding for new projects.*

Overall, conferences and exhibitions are powerful tools that can help women entrepreneurs grow their businesses and progress, supporting them on their path to success.

Chapter 10
'*Through the Garden Gate*' and social innovations

The *Through the Garden Gate* Program

Linda Jones alongside Mahbooba, in Parwan province during a 2007 "Through the Garden Gate" program visit.

Before we delve into the *Through the Garden Gate* program, which was founded in 2007, I want to take you back to late 2003 and early 2004, when I first met Dr Linda Jones. With bright eyes and a warm smile that always graced her lips, Linda seemed to embody the spirit of nature itself. Our meeting took place on a beautiful day at the council's headquarters. Linda spoke enthusiastically about the activities of a fledgling organization and asked questions that felt like those of an old friend. From that moment, I realized that she had a deep commitment to social development, particularly for the people of Afghanistan, and specifically for women.

This social development dream ultimately came true in 2007 with the launch of the *Through the Garden Gate* program, a project that was shaped through the efforts and love of Linda and her team, including Helen Loftin, Catherine Subrevega, and Lana Moo.

Helen, as the program director, was an exceptional person with a kind heart and a strong will. With her attention to detail, she was always seeking innovative ways to improve the lives of Afghan women. Helen

Helen Loftin representing Afghan women in Canada

was not only a director but also a friend and advocate for rural women, representing Afghan women at international conferences – inspiring everyone with her passion for her work.

Catherine, the program manager in Afghanistan, stood courageously against all challenges and obstacles. With a deep understanding of the culture and fluency in the local sign language, she established a strong connection with the people and energetically advanced the project. Catherine, with her sincerity and dedication, was always there, both for her team and the Afghan women, providing them with hope and motivation.

Lana Moo, an expert in agriculture, was also a valuable member of the team. With her technical expertise and extensive experience in agriculture, she played a major role in improving living conditions and farming practices in rural Afghanistan. Lena, with her perseverance and high motivation, along with Catherine, played a key role in achieving the goals of *Through the Garden Gate* in the country and helped build trust and cooperation with the local community.

Ann Gordon, through her tireless efforts and unwavering passion for empowering women, established a regional network connecting women from Afghanistan, Pakistan, and Tajikistan – the Regional Women's Economic Network (RWEN). With unparalleled enthusiasm, she launched multiple programs in these three countries. These programs included workshops on the production chain system, from production to market entry, exhibitions, visits to production stages, and training on high-quality production. She believed that through active participation, women could build a brighter future for themselves and their communities.

In the AWBC office, Zainab Wahidi, Evaluation Director at the MEDA organization, is alongside Mahbooba during the monitoring and evaluation of the "Through the Garden Gate" project.

Zainab Wahidi, who worked with precision and expertise in the evaluation department, played another vital role in the program. With her sharp eye and attention to detail, she always sought to assess the quality and impact of the programs in the best possible way. Zainab, with her positive outlook and high motivation, identified the strengths and weaknesses of the projects and provided constructive feedback, paving the way for improvement and growth. Her passion and commitment reminded everyone that even small steps on the path to progress can have a huge impact on the lives of rural women.

Mari acted as a bridge between the team and the farmer women. With her outstanding communication skills and a heart full of love and empathy, she was able to effectively gain the trust and support of the community. She was always ready to listen to concerns and find solutions to them. Mari, with patience and dedication, would listen to the worries of rural women and relay their needs to the team. She believed that strong communication and mutual respect were the foundation of success, and with this belief, she played a key role in creating a friendly and supportive environment for the program.

Finally, Nabila Osmani, Mari, Laila Arab Shahee, Zaiton, Lailuma Abassy, Parinaz, Durkhanai, and many other inspiring and hard-working women played an active role in various educational and social programs in the fields of social development, trade techniques, and agriculture. They were individuals who, with a deep love for people and faith in the power of education, created positive changes in the lives of rural women. Their tireless and persistent efforts in education and empowerment are admirable and will continue to inspire future generations.

These women, with their determination, travelled long and difficult paths to reach various villages. Wherever they went, the women farmers and their families greeted them warmly, regardless of gender. This reception not only reflected the respect and appreciation the community had for these educated women, but also sparked hope and motivation in the hearts of the people.

The women farmers, with enthusiasm and love, were part of the wider *Through the Garden Gate* family, who, with faith and hope in a brighter future, also paved the way for the empowerment of women. They turned fertile lands and lush gardens into flourishing spaces for growth. Every day, with the sunrise, they woke up and planted the seeds of life with their capable hands and hopeful hearts. These women, with their commitment and resilience in the face of challenges, produced high-quality products and simultaneously passed on agricultural traditions and customs to future generations. The spirit of cooperation and mutual support was one of this

Mahbooba and Laila – meeting with the community to learn from the community.

network's prominent features. Whenever one of them faced a problem, the others would immediately come to their aid. Harvest days became a celebration of colours and scents, bringing families together. In these moments, joy and excitement reached its peak, and the atmosphere was filled with laughter and happiness.

Through the Garden Gate became a garden for growth and solidarity, a place where the long-held dreams of rural Afghan women came true and provided an opportunity for them to flourish. These home gardens, which have now become permanent sources of income for families, have not only become spaces for learning and acquiring new skills in agriculture and gardening, but also centres for the exchange of experiences and knowledge. Through cooperation and solidarity, women share their skills and expertise with each other, strengthening their unity and mutual support. To this day, this project has enabled women to empower themselves through sustainable agriculture, improve their lives and their families, and play a significant role in their communities. The program has directly impacted the lives of 2,250 women and more than 10,000 members of their families.

These heroic women played vital roles not only in agriculture but also in other aspects of life. They managed families with wisdom and insight, having a significant impact on raising their children too. Their upbringing, based on love, respect, and human values, nurtured responsible and compassionate individuals. The future that these women believed in was not only for themselves but also for the entire community in which they lived. Through their tireless efforts, they showed that with hope, love, and solidarity, any obstacle can be overcome, and they paved the way for a brighter and more prosperous future for all.

Women farmers learned how to find new ways to improve their economic situation, enabling them to farm their land more effectively. However, the high costs of purchasing raw materials always left them feeling powerless. Then they formed savings and credit groups, now each member was able to save for their needs and take loans in times of necessity.

One such savings group began collecting small savings and soon women farmers like Farideh happily realized that now she could use her savings to purchase agricultural supplies. Another woman named Robabeh used her savings to buy livestock, and Zarmena decided to use her savings to pay for her children's education. Day by day, the number of happy and empowered women in the group grew.

All members of this rural group were aware of their individual savings, the total group savings, and the amount of loans given to members. This transparency and cooperation allowed the group to move forward with great care and excellent management. They not only improved their own lives but also helped others to walk the path of growth and progress.

Identifying rural needs

Within the framework of the *Through the Garden Gate* program, the Afghanistan Women's Business Council played an active role as leaders of social development, particularly in rural areas. To improve understanding of how rural and traditional communities evolve, the council selected villages and analysed their history, deeply examining the cultural impacts on society. This research not only helped understand the fundamental priorities of the community but also emphasized preserving and strengthening traditional identities through cultural initiatives.

Evaluating the state of education in villages and increasing access to educational programs that match community needs was also an important activity of this program. Analysing local businesses and economic conditions, especially whether the economy was more agricultural or focused on handicrafts, was critical. These studies explored the types of agricultural products and their potential for development.

Understanding rural values and beliefs and their role in shaping cultural identity was also emphasized as part of the project. Analysing these factors helped us better understand the challenges and opportunities in traditional rural communities and identify the appropriate priorities for their development. This crucial step plays a vital role in improving living standards and achieving sustainable community development.

During our visits to the villages to identify people's needs, we often encountered a group of men. These men were typically local elders, unemployed individuals, or retirees. They often emphasized

Catherine Subrevega, next to Mahbooba; engaging with local community members to identify needs and promote women's participation in rural development initiatives.

that job opportunities should first be provided to men, and only then to women, showing a strict attitude toward women's roles outside the home. However, after various discussions, we were able to convince them that women, even with household responsibilities, could help themselves and their families by learning social and economic skills.

In discussions with local leaders, they expressed concerns that women's work outside the home might promote Western culture in Afghanistan. Furthermore, their sense of pride and responsibility prevented them from supporting women in markets or engaging with unrelated men.

Through continuous dialogues and convincing arguments, the men eventually compromised, agreeing that if women wanted to work outside the home, these spaces should be exclusively for women, and men's access should be prohibited. They also emphasized that any teacher instructing women should be a woman. However, through effective awareness-raising, men can actively support women both at home and in society.

In discussions among powerful women's groups, they believed that opportunities for women's income were extremely limited. They argued that the implementation of the *Through the Garden Gate* program would significantly increase employment and help families meet their needs, boosting hope for the future. They believed that when women became economically empowered, they would play an important role in achieving peace in their communities – which would lead to more work and less violence. Through such consultation we were able to help women farmers not only set up businesses but also enhance their abilities to care for their families at the same time.

Innovative tools and techniques

Rural programs like these also introduce useful new tools and techniques to communities – such as drip irrigation systems and solar dryers, which greatly improved the efficiency and quality of agricultural practices. These innovations allowed women to conserve water, reduce crop waste, and sell their produce at higher prices. Additionally, community savings funds were established to provide financial support for women in need and encourage financial independence.

The formation of sales agents and the training of women farmers focused on enhancing their communication skills, particularly to facilitate connections with markets and input suppliers, as well as improving interactions among women farmers. This approach enabled the sales agents to identify the best customers and implement effective marketing strategies for the products, which ultimately had a significant positive impact not only on the agents themselves but also on other women farmers. Sales agents were typically selected from among older women, as this choice was more socially and familiarly acceptable. Furthermore, their relatively fewer family responsibilities compared to younger women made their participation in these programs easier. Additionally, the transparent work of these women in the community earned them greater respect and credibility.

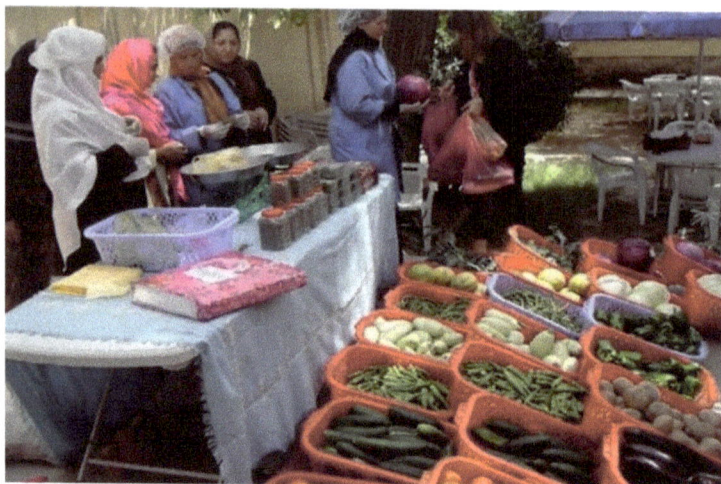

Mahbooba at the Women Farmers' Sunday Market in Kabul. In this striking image from a Kabul neighbourhood, women from nine villages in Parwan province, alongside their sales agents, proudly showcased and sold their handmade and natural goods. Their presence in the heart of the city highlights the resilience of Afghan women.

Another goal of this training was to provide new ideas on business, management, and the essential elements needed for establishing rural businesses. Furthermore, the training equipped women farmers with the skills to accurately record and manage their farm income and expenses, enabling them to access markets more effectively and succeed in selling their products.

The *Through the Garden Gate* program empowered rural women by providing them with valuable agricultural and financial knowledge, strengthening their social networks, and boosting their confidence and economic independence. Through the program's ongoing support and the shared success stories, women in rural Afghanistan are transforming their lives and contributing to the sustainable development of their communities.

Empowering rural women through literacy

In addition to training in agricultural and business skills under the program, women have been empowered to learn to read and write in their own language. They then take on the responsibility of creating employment and production opportunities for others in the country though learning and teaching.

Rural women receiving literacy education based on the belief that educating a mother is educating the community, and investing in women's education is the key to achieving a successful and sustainable society.

The establishment of literacy courses, savings and lending groups, and encouraging women to participate in local council advisory meetings are among the achievements that have enabled rural women to initiate their own educational programs, mobilize, and oversee savings and lending activities. The literacy courses organized in coordination with the Literacy Department of the Ministry of Education created a support system for the national educational framework through training courses that enhance fundamental literacy skills, agricultural and business expertise, and effectively support community mobilization. This program effectively led to the economic participation and improved economic status of women.

The design and publication of illustrated books was another innovative educational method. Illustrated books were designed and printed by the Afghanistan Women's Business Council – their goal was to teach development techniques and literacy skills to female farmers. The books were specifically designed for illiterate women and provided practical information through images, charts, and simple explanations. This educational tool facilitated learning and strengthened agricultural skills in rural areas while encouraging women to learn reading and writing, which helped empower and advance them in society.

Reflections on the effectiveness of programs that focus on empowering rural women

Experience Sharing and Emotional Support: These programs allow participants to share their experiences in dealing with challenges, helping others feel less isolated and emotionally supported. By learning from the mistakes and successes of others, individuals can adopt new strategies for overcoming difficulties.

Strengthening Social Connections and Problem-Solving: Public counselling and shared learning experiences can help participants build stronger social bonds and improve communication with others. Sharing practical solutions and successful strategies allows participants to tackle problems more effectively by incorporating diverse perspectives.

Social Support and Community Engagement: In times of difficulty, social support becomes crucial. These programs offer opportunities for participants to support each other, creating a sense of community. Community participation in decision-making and social awareness activities fosters collective action for social improvement and personal development.

The Through the Garden Gate initiative was an innovative program that, in addition to agricultural training, also provided financial education such as saving and investment strategies for women and young girls. Unlike traditional programs that primarily focused on domestic skills, the MEDA organization introduced a new approach by integrating both technical and financial education for women in rural Afghanistan.

Key outcomes include:

Increased Involvement in Profitable Ventures: While women in rural areas were primarily engaged in low-income agricultural activities, the MEDA program helped them learn new skills, leading to participation in more profitable agricultural activities.

Economic Empowerment and Independence: Through training in both agriculture and finance, women were able to manage their resources better and contribute more significantly to their families' economic and social lives. This empowerment not only increased family income but also helped women become more independent and active in their communities.

Long-Term Impact: The success of the program in areas like Parwan province has led to its spread to neighbouring regions where women are using the skills they've learned to improve their livelihoods.

Stories of success

The success stories of women like Nasrin and Shirin illustrate the profound impact of these programs. Nasrin, who learned modern agricultural techniques, now runs her farm professionally and has increased her family's income. Similarly, Shirin has used the income from her agricultural activities to support her children's education and purchase livestock, which contributes to her family's financial stability. Both women have also gained confidence and a sense of accomplishment, seeing their families and communities benefit from the new skills they have acquired.

A story of hope and effort for a brighter future

Through the Garden Gate has provided unique opportunities for women farmers. This program not only cultivates the land but also profoundly changes the lives of women. In a MEDA annual report Nasrin shares her life story with passion and enthusiasm.

Nasrin bought a cow that now sustains her family – a woman who turned determination into success, rising from hardship to confidently shaping her future.

With eyes full of hope, Nasrin says, "Now, I have achieved my dreams. Years ago, when I thought about my future, I never imagined I would arrive here. I use the techniques I learned from MEDA and manage our small piece of land in a completely professional manner. Now I know how to prepare my land, water my plants, control weeds, and harvest and store our produce. This knowledge has empowered me to prepare jams, pickles, and dried vegetables for the winter. By selling my excess produce, I have been able to buy the things I need."

She continues, "My life is now very organized. I can manage my time to work on the land and attend trainings. I also have time for my family and relatives, which is very valuable to me. I am not just a farmer; I am also a businesswoman. When I see my children walking towards school with their backpacks, I feel very proud as a mother because I have fulfilled my responsibility to provide them with an education."

Nasrin adds with gratitude, "Additionally, I was able to buy a cow and use it for my family's livelihood. This cow not only provides us with food but also gives me strength and confidence. MEDA showed me how to make the best use of available resources and improve my life."

Nasrin's story is a tale of hope and effort; it is the story of a woman who, with courage and determination, has reached her dreams and today not only works on her land but also cultivates a garden of hope and aspiration in her heart. With faith in a brighter future, she walks alongside her family, working to build a better life. *Through the Garden Gate*, helped her and others like her plant the seeds of hope in the soil and reap the rewards day by day.

"Now, all of my children go to school, and this is my greatest joy. Every day, when I see them walking towards school with their new backpacks and enthusiasm, my heart fills with gratitude. This was exactly the dream I held in my heart for so many years: an education and a bright future for each of them. Today, I look towards the future with more confidence than ever because the knowledge and techniques I learned from this project will shine like a light in my life.

With the income I earn from farming, I have been able to buy a cow, sheep, and chickens. This not only symbolizes success for me but also provides a way to support my family's livelihood. I also bought a pushcart for my son, which he uses to sell the produce from our garden. He works with such enthusiasm, and that fills me with great pride. I have also learned new techniques such as greenhouse planting and building trellises for grapes. These skills have helped me harvest better produce. My dream is to someday gather enough resources to invest in building an underground storage for vegetables. I know that by doing this, my income will increase, and my life will become more comfortable and secure.

I am sincerely grateful to MEDA for their commitment to helping women like me. We are truly fortunate, as with their support, we can now move toward a brighter future, and this is just the beginning of our story."

From farm to university – a story of courage and transformation

Interview with Ms. Shabana, Group Leader of Farmers in the Through the Garden Gate Program, August 1, 2023

In the green, mountainous villages of Afghanistan, in 2007, the simple and challenging life of a young woman named Shabana transformed in an astonishing way. Shabana was selected as the group leader of farmers in the *Through the Garden Gate* program in a village that was slowly changing due to internal conflicts. This selection was not just a personal victory, but a symbol of significant change within a traditional and conservative society.

With resolute determination and a heart full of hope, Shabana began her work and quickly immersed herself in a new world of activities and challenges. Collaborating with the program and the Afghanistan Women's Business Council, she engaged in practical and theoretical training in agriculture, business, social development, and management. Shabana seized every opportunity to learn and grow, acquiring valuable skills along the way.

Shabana's efforts did not stop there. With unparalleled perseverance, she successfully earned a bachelor's degree from the Faculty of Language and Literature in Parwan Province. This achievement was a testament to her endless will and determination. After her studies, Shabana worked as a social worker with non-governmental organizations, contributing to the improvement of her community's conditions. She became a source of inspiration for many women and men in her village, using her experiences to help others.

Through her sales income, Shabana was able to continue her education and raise her children with love and care. While participating in the program, she had three children and now has seven: four daughters and three sons. However, when she talks about her daughters, her eyes fill with tears. Her daughters, who once had big dreams of pursuing education, have now returned home and been deprived of schooling under the Taliban regime. Two of her older daughters have graduated from school, while her third daughter has now dropped out due to the Taliban's restrictions.

However, thanks to the opportunities provided by the *Through the Garden Gate* empowerment program, Shabana was able to improve her family's economic situation. With this economic improvement, she kept her children away from domestic violence and provided them with pens instead of guns. In doing so, Shabana gifted her family with love and peace, bringing warmth and tranquillity into their home.

One step forward, two steps back! – women's participation in decision-making

One of the major achievements of the *Through the Garden Gate* program has been the empowerment of representatives from women's farming groups in rural areas. These women have played a significant role in the economy of their families and communities. They have demonstrated that women are not only influential in managing households and raising children but can also actively participate in key decision-making processes that shape the future of their communities. These women have achieved remarkable success by enhancing agriculture and engaging in the value chain – from preparation and planting to marketing.

Promoting rural women's leadership requires comprehensive programs to empower and strengthen their participation in decision-making processes within their communities. In the program, fundamental strategies for nurturing rural women's leadership are clearly and tangibly visible. Sadly, when the Taliban took control of Afghanistan, Shabana's world, along with that of many other women, changed horrifically. The prohibitions and stringent restrictions placed her in a difficult position.

Despite this, with courage and iron will, Shabana continued her secret activities and tirelessly provided essential services to the women of her village. In the depths of darkness and away from prying eyes, she has become a true hero, demonstrating that even in the toughest conditions, hope and determination can transform into a guiding light.

Shabana joyfully sent me a photo of her finished products, saying, "Look, our products are ready for market." Her husband loaded the goods early in the morning and took them to the Kabul market to sell at a better price. This couple, working side by side with unwavering determination, exemplifies cooperation and resilience in the face of adversity.

The lives of Shabana's three young daughters, who aspired to build a bright future, were severely affected. They spent their days dreaming of education and a better tomorrow, but now they are confined to their home, where only the sound of shattered dreams can be heard. Their parents, with weary hearts and hardworking hands, spend their days in the fields and their nights filled with worry and sorrow. With a broken heart and tearful eyes, Shabana reminisces about a future that was once full of light and hope, now a bitter memory. She is in search of hope, constantly asking herself, "Will there ever come a day when my daughters can return to school and achieve their dreams?"

Shabana's story is not just that of a successful woman; it is a testament to human strength and resilience. Through her struggles and sacrifices, she proved that no power can break the spirit and resolve of a person, inspiring many women and men around her to look towards a brighter more hopeful future too.

Chapter 11
Badam Bagh-e Kabul – beyond almonds

Empowerment and hope for Afghan women

In the heart of Kabul, in a green and peaceful place called Badam Bagh, a real and remarkable story of change and empowerment for women took shape. This was not just an ordinary garden; it was a place where profound social and economic transformations occurred. Spanning 260 hectares, Badam Bagh served as a research and agricultural centre, not only promoting Afghanistan's agricultural products but also acting as a bridge between culture and global markets, where every product carried a story of effort and hope.

In Badam Bagh, Kabul women are leading a transformative agricultural project. Through cultivating and marketing produce, they gain technical skills and income opportunities. Mahboba as CEO of the council, oversees the process, ensuring quality and empowering women with sustainable employment and vocational training.

In this garden, Afghan women were writing a different story. Among the flowers and trees, they became empowered to not only manage agricultural lands but also build their own small businesses, showing the world that they too had the ability to enter the world of trade and production. The Afghanistan Women's Business Council, in collaboration with the Ministry of Agriculture and Livestock, provided them with a golden opportunity: training that encompassed everything from agricultural principles and harvesting to financial management and marketing. These trainings enabled women to achieve independence amid economic and social crises and establish businesses that supported not only themselves but their families as well.

At first glance, Badam Bagh might seem like just a research centre, but it was a place where emerging businesses flourished. Women in this garden harvested fruits and vegetables with their determined hands, then carefully sorted and packaged them for the market. In this process, they not only sold products but also created new job opportunities and helped reduce waste. Some of the products even went to women in need, hospitals, and refugee camps – humanitarian aid reaching far-off areas.

For many women in Badam Bagh, it was more than just farming; it was a journey toward self-sufficiency and empowerment. Many used the income from selling the products to buy basic items to start their small businesses. Some even managed to begin processing their own products, thus finding a place in new markets. These changes not only improved the economic status of these women but also transformed their social lives. As emerging and independent entrepreneurs, women found an opportunity to educate themselves and improve their families' living conditions.

Women not only gather the produce but also skilfully sort and package it for market distribution.

Alongside these transformations, the unity and cooperation among women's business unions in various provinces of Afghanistan, especially in Parwan, led to the creation of a network of business opportunities and training for women. These unions not only strengthened women's economic and social capabilities but also helped promote modern agricultural practices under women's management.

But this was not the end of the story! In Parwan, in the heart of Charikar city, a new business centre for women entrepreneurs was established. This centre became the first communication hub for women in Afghanistan, offering a unique opportunity for them to learn new skills in trade and agriculture. Exhibitions were held in this centre, where women could showcase their products and benefit from each other's experience.

In this challenging but hopeful journey, Badam Bagh was not just a point on the map; it became a symbol of the strength, will, and effort of Afghan women to improve their lives and their community. Here, women built a better future with their own hands, a future filled with new opportunities, hope, and independence.

Mahboba as CEO of the council, stands alongside Nabila Osmani, the council's deputy, as they explain the distribution process to representatives from one of the camps for displaced families. A promise that what's being delivered is not only food, but a powerful message – you are seen, you are heard, and you matter.

Some of the fresh, carefully harvested products from Badam Bagh made its way beyond the garden – carried not just in boxes, but in the spirit of compassion. Distribution was more than a logistical act; it was a gesture of humanity as goods reached the hands of those in need – patients in hospitals, families in remote villages, and displaced people in refugee camps – bringing with them not just nourishment, but hope.

Reflections on the impacts of emerging business enterprises

Women's emerging businesses, with their unique characteristics, play a significant and influential role in improving the lives of individuals and communities. These impacts are particularly evident for women in areas such as self-sufficiency, job creation, poverty reduction, and enhanced quality of life – pivotal in economic and social transformation.

__Self-sufficiency__: Emerging businesses contribute to reducing dependency on foreign imports by focusing on innovative products and services. This enhances the economic security of countries and protects individuals from global market instability.

__Job Creation__: These businesses promote economic growth by generating new job opportunities, leading to increased employment rates and improved income levels, which in turn contribute to national economic development.

__Poverty Reduction__: By offering more job opportunities and raising income levels, these businesses play a significant role in reducing poverty and improving the standard of living for individuals.

__Access to Education for Children__: These businesses help improve educational opportunities for children, contributing to the development of future generations.

__Improving Women's Quality of Life__: Emerging businesses support women's participation in agriculture and commerce, boosting their economic independence and overall quality of life.

__Job Creation for Women__: Through agricultural production, food processing, and handicrafts, these businesses create new employment opportunities for women.

__Education for Women__: By providing specialized training in agriculture, business management, and risk analysis, these businesses help enhance the skills and knowledge of women.

__Women's Management Experience__: Women's involvement in agricultural programs and managing family livelihoods demonstrates their effective role in leading and executing economic projects.

__Modern Agricultural Culture Led by Women__: These businesses promote modern agricultural practices managed by women, expanding their roles as leaders and experts in the field.

__Promoting Collaboration Among Women__: Emerging businesses encourage the sharing of knowledge and experiences among women involved in agriculture, empowering them as key players in social and economic development.

A story of hope and sacrifice

Mrs. Humaira Shakiba is a woman who rose from adversity and proved to everyone that nothing can stop the will of an Afghan woman. This is her story – the story of a woman who, amid crises and challenges, gave hope and a strong will to her own life and the women of her country. Once a supervisor in the Badam Bagh program, today she walks a new path full of responsibility as the CEO of the Afghanistan Women's Business Council.

Humaira's journey began in Badam Bagh where she spent her days alongside women farmers and entrepreneurs. A turning point in her life, she knew that in order to change the lives of women, she had to take the first step herself. From the very beginning, with patience and perseverance, she taught women how to become self-sufficient and make progress in the economic and social worlds. For her, Badam Bagh was not just a workplace; it was a place where Afghan women could rediscover their self-belief and unlock their true power.

Her personal life has never been without challenges. She is the mother of six children, and her husband tragically passed away due to a heart attack, leaving her to raise their children on her own. Despite the family pressures and being a widow, she never gave up on her efforts to advance herself and the women's community. During her time as a supervisor, she also managed to obtain her university degree. This achievement, despite the difficult circumstances, demonstrates further her strong resolve.

With endless motivation and a heart full of dreams, Mrs. Shakiba continued her work. In the face of economic and cultural challenges, she decided to strengthen her managerial skills. With hard work and determination, she became one of the prominent managers in the program. As a supervisor, she created new opportunities for women, ranging from agricultural training to marketing and financial management skills, helping them enter the world of business and become self-sufficient.

Over time, Humaira reached a higher position and was appointed as the CEO of the Afghanistan Women's Business Council. This heavy responsibility placed a great burden on her, but she never strayed from her path. In this role, she not only worked to develop educational and empowerment programs but also became a role model for Afghan women, always emphasizing that any woman can achieve a significant place in the economic and social world, as long as she believes in herself and her abilities.

However, with the return of the Taliban to Afghanistan, the situation for her and other women became extremely difficult. New restrictions halted all women's activities in various fields. But Humaira never surrendered. Instead of despairing, she decided to find new ways to continue her work. She knew that even within these restrictions, she had to find a way to serve women. She kept searching and working to provide new job opportunities and effective training for women.

In these tough circumstances, many Afghan women are struggling just to meet basic life needs, such as securing bread for the day and night. In such a situation, maintaining connections with women and helping them progress in their paths is of great importance. Humaira understands that by promoting entrepreneurship and encouraging women in economic activities, job opportunities can be created. She uses modern marketing methods and organizes limited exhibitions to help women showcase their products in the market, improving their livelihoods and providing opportunities to escape poverty in the face of hardship.

For this purpose, she turned her home office into a workspace. In this small office, she offers consultations, provides training, and helps women display their products in limited exhibitions. These exhibitions give women the chance to benefit from each other's experiences and introduce their products.

Additionally, she is working to secretly connect women with NGOs that offer confidential training programs, enabling them to acquire new skills and make progress in business and agriculture – never missing any opportunity to empower women in the most difficult conditions.

Since entering the world of women's empowerment, Humaira Shakiba has always believed that education and equal opportunities can create a bright future for women. However, today, with Afghanistan under Taliban control, her heart is heavier than ever. When she looks at her daughter, her heart aches. Her daughter, once eager to go to school, can no longer take a step toward education due to new restrictions.

She remains strongly hopeful that one day the situation will change, and Afghan girls and women will once again be able to study in schools and universities, work in various professions, and live independent and successful lives. She firmly believes that Afghan women have limitless abilities and can excel in every field of life; they just need the right opportunities and conditions.

Humaira never gives up on hope. She still remembers the days when Afghan women used to go to markets, stand together, and engage in discussions. She lives with the hope that one day, Afghan women will be given opportunities that benefit not only themselves but also their communities.

She wakes up every day with a heart full of hope and continues her work in her small office. She knows that every step she takes for women brings her closer to a better day and remembers the days when Afghan women used to go to school, work in agriculture with their own hands, and contribute to building a better society together. Humaira Shakiba still believes in this dream and hopes that one day all these opportunities will be restored for Afghan women.

Chapter 12
Promoting women's empowerment in Kabul and the provinces

The *House-to-House* Educational Program

The *House-to-House* educational program, initiated by the board members and the executive team of the Afghanistan Women's Business Council (AWBC), was launched with the goal of enhancing educational capacity and empowering women in fifteen districts across Kabul city. These courses helped women acquire essential skills, enabling them to improve the quality of life for themselves and their families. The primary goal of the program was to support 500 women entrepreneurs in small and medium-sized businesses, with each of these women acting as cultural and skills representatives by inviting three other women to participate in the training.

Mahbooba with Mari Enayat, designer and quality control manager, of the *House-to-House* educational program – playing a key role in professional development, personal growth, effective communication, and positive networking within the community.

As a result, a total of 1,500 women from Kabul directly and indirectly benefited from the program.

These achievements not only impacted the lives of the direct participants but also had positive effects on families and various districts of Kabul. In total, 7,500 women reaped the benefits of this program. These successes contributed to the spread of skills and the passing of knowledge to future generations, fostering the individual and collective empowerment of women in society.

In addition to promoting individual empowerment, the project also focuses on the production of handicrafts, equipping Afghan women entrepreneurs with skills and abilities that enhance their success in the business sector. The program further creates new business ties between Afghan women's small and medium-sized enterprises and their European counterparts by organizing trade missions, thus helping to increase economic interactions and attract investments.

The specific goals of this project include strengthening and developing the capacities of AWBC members in the production and distribution of high-quality products, supporting women-owned small and medium-sized enterprises in the import/export processes, and enhancing AWBC's services to Afghan women entrepreneurs. Moreover, creating business networks with Latvian and Greek companies and exploring business opportunities in the European market are also among the objectives of this project.

The fulfillment of these goals will lead to new international contacts and the development of business relationships with European counterparts, improving Afghanistan's global image. The project also strengthens the private sector, particularly women-owned small and medium-sized enterprises, providing an opportunity for the development of new businesses.

This program has not only contributed to the growth and strengthening of initial efforts but will also be passed on as a valuable legacy to future generations. We are collectively proud that this program has played a key role in developing women's personalities and professionalism, fostering positive connections, creating effective networks within the community, and, overall, building a bright and hopeful future.

The first steps of the Afghanistan Women's Business Council (AWBC) in this innovative *House-to-House* program were taken with great enthusiasm. The main focus of this initiative was to support women entrepreneurs in Afghanistan, particularly in rural and urban areas with limited access to markets. AWBC, with a clear objective and a broader mission, worked to empower women-led businesses by providing essential tools, knowledge, and connections for their success in the market. This programme not only helped women progress in their entrepreneurial journey but also laid the foundation for a significant transformation in Afghanistan's economy and social empowerment.

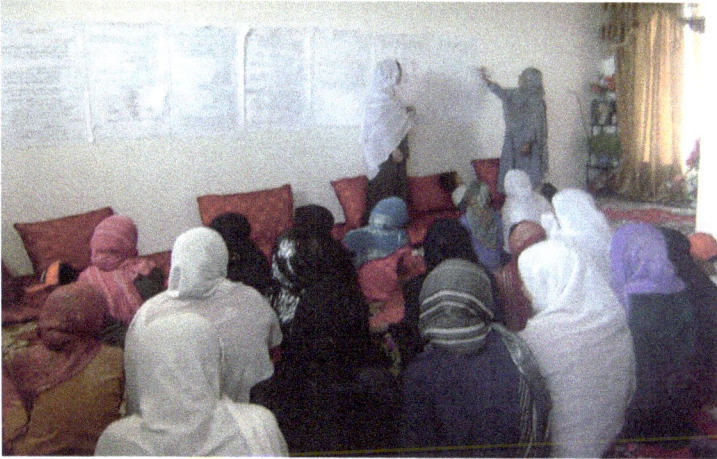

An example of the training provided through the *"House-to-House"* education program

The primary goal of this initiative was to provide Afghan women with business and marketing skills so they could manage their businesses more effectively. The project, with a focus on helping women meet market needs, improve product design, and increase their access to broader markets, was specifically designed to bring about positive and sustainable change.

AWBC launched this initiative directly to address the challenges faced by Afghan women, especially those in rural areas who were struggling with livelihood issues for themselves and their families. Thousands of Afghan women, particularly those working from home, were facing severe difficulties in generating enough income to meet their needs. The *House-to-House* program was designed to change this situation and strengthen the economic capacities of these women, enabling them to expand their businesses and compete with confidence in the national market.

Through this project, AWBC took significant steps to reach housebound women in both rural and urban areas, with the focus on increasing their income. It is noteworthy that AWBC exceeded expectations by helping 1,500 women to double their income.

A key component of this innovative programme was the creation of a network of 30 female vendors who worked closely with women producers. These vendors effectively facilitated the communication between rural women producers and the urban markets of Kabul, particularly in the embroidery and clothing industries. This network established vital links between producers and key market players, ensuring that women's products were presented to a wider audience. The vendors who played a crucial role in connecting housebound women with urban markets also played a key role in bridging the gap between rural producers and urban consumers, helping to expand the scope of these women's businesses. The initiative also included extensive training in areas such as quality control and product development to ensure that products met market standards and consumer needs.

Another example of *House-to-House* educational training, designed and monitored by the AWBC – empowering women across Kabul by building skills, supporting entrepreneurship, and strengthening communities from within.

Additionally, the AWBC programme focused on providing business and technical training in areas such as design, marketing, and business management, helping Afghan women achieve short-term successes while equipping them with the skills and knowledge necessary to maintain and grow their businesses in a competitive market.

As a result, it was clear that AWBC's interventions had a profound and positive impact on the lives of Afghan women. The income of women active in the embroidery industry and other value chains had more than doubled, and the network of vendors continued to expand rapidly, directly contributing to the development and expansion of the project into more rural areas. AWBC's tireless efforts not only had a lasting economic impact but also created positive changes in the lives of these women by addressing their immediate income needs and providing the skills and connections required for building sustainable businesses.

This project represented an innovative approach in which AWBC, by offering specialised training and helping women directly connect their products with the market, was able to significantly improve the livelihoods of many entrepreneurial women. Through innovative methods such as using female vendors and focusing on long-term sustainability, AWBC is creating tangible changes and a deep transformation in the lives of Afghan women. The impact of this project continues to evolve and expand, creating a bright and hopeful future for the women involved.

Today, we are witnessing significant progress in women's businesses at various levels, and these achievements need to be documented comprehensively so that we can assess the progress of these changes and help expand these successes in the future.

Chapter 13
Reflections on historic transformative programs

The formation of the Afghanistan Women's Business Federation

In the intricate history of women's entrepreneurship in Afghanistan, the establishment of the Afghanistan Women's Business Federation marks an unprecedented milestone. This federation not only paved a new path for Afghan women entrepreneurs but also laid a strong foundation for the economic growth and prosperity of women in a country that has long faced numerous challenges.

Efforts to create an organized platform to support women entrepreneurs began when the Afghanistan Women's Business Council, comprising 23 active unions from diverse sectors such as carpet weaving, tailoring, embroidery, food industries, transportation, and construction, came together. This council, in close collaboration with the Afghan Women's Business Association sought to establish a more robust and inclusive structure to support women in economic fields.

After months of consultations and coordination, a proposal was put forward to establish a comprehensive institution to align and integrate the business activities of Afghan women. The support of an international organization and the formation of a transitional board were significant steps toward the federation's establishment. In this process, these two prominent institutions – the Afghanistan Women's Business Council and the Afghanistan Women's Business Association – played a pivotal role in managing this transitional phase and worked tirelessly to achieve this major objective.

After the initial structures were solidified, the final election process was launched to select the official board of directors for the federation. This election was conducted transparently under the supervision of the same international organization that had overseen the project from its inception.

Ultimately, nine board members were elected from a pool of candidates to lead the newly established federation toward growth and development. Among them, the appointment of a capable Lithuanian woman as the first president of the Afghanistan Women's Business Federation was an unprecedented and symbolic move, reflecting the federation's approach to leveraging international expertise for the empowerment of Afghan women in trade and business. Accepting the responsibility for a three-year term, this committed leader worked diligently to strengthen the foundation of the federation and pave the way for its progress.

Over time, the Afghanistan Women's Business Federation evolved from a nascent organization into an influential institution that provided exceptional opportunities for future female leaders in Afghanistan. Despite facing numerous challenges, the federation implemented a variety of programs that created a platform for empowering women in various economic fields.

The presence of distinguished individuals within this federation tells an inspiring story of per-severance, struggle, and success – one that must be documented. Each person who took steps in this journey contributed to laying the strong groundwork for the growth of Afghan women entrepreneurs. Today, we witness the fruits of these efforts.

Looking back, it becomes clear that the Afghanistan Women's Business Federation was not merely an organization but a transformative movement toward women's empowerment. The seeds sown in those early days have now grown into towering trees, bearing fruit for Afghan women entrepreneurs across various economic and social domains.

As a symbol of Afghan women's determination, this federation continues to inspire a generation of female entrepreneurs striving for a brighter and more hopeful future. Challenges will always persist, but the achievements realized thus far stand as a testament to the boundless capabilities of the women of this land on the path of development and progress.

Unprecedented membership to the Afghanistan Chamber of Commerce & Industry

The Afghanistan Chamber of Commerce & Industry has a long history of serving the private sector, dating back 92 years. In 1931, Afghan traders established the Commercial Arbitration Assembly for the first time to address business disputes and coordinate their activities. This assembly later evolved into the Afghanistan Chamber of Commerce & Industry creating provincial representations to advocate for the private sector. The Chamber's law was approved and ratified in 2009, defining it as a fully independent, non-governmental, non-political, and non-profit entity.

This marked a step toward greater collaboration between the private sector and the government in creating a conducive business environment, driven by the private sector across the country. Consequently, this process established the Afghanistan Chamber of Commerce & Industry as a key institution in the development and promotion of the country's economy, playing a significant role in strengthening commercial infrastructure. With the enactment of the Chamber's law in 2009, it became recognized as an independent and credible authority in commercial and industrial matters, fulfilling its role in regulating and improving business conditions at both national and local levels.

Given the illustrious history of the Afghanistan Chamber of Commerce & Industry, this institution has played a crucial role in the growth and development of the private sector. However, until 2002, women's presence in this institution had not been seriously considered. Fortunately, since then, women's entry into managerial and economic fields has allowed the Afghanistan Women's Business Council to achieve group membership in the Afghanistan Chamber of Commerce & Industry for the first time. This historic membership marks a turning point in both the history of the Chamber and the economic history of the country, as it enables women to officially and effectively participate in economic decision-making and influence the country's policies and business programs.

This achievement reflects significant progress toward gender equality and the enhancement of women's roles in the Afghan economy, clearly demonstrating the social and economic changes in the country since the early 21st century. Through this membership, the Afghanistan Women's Business Council has not only strengthened the position of women in the economic sphere but has also contributed to increasing confidence and improving the level of economic activities in the country.

A symbol of solidarity and women's advancement

Our vibrant presence, a group of active women, including three members of the Board of the Afghanistan Women's Business Council, on the Board of the Afghanistan Chamber of Commerce & Industry truly symbolizes solidarity and the power of women in business. In an environment often dominated by men, we participated as a group of women in several election cycles of the Chamber and, with a majority of votes, were elected as board members.

The Afghanistan Women's Business Council, as the first collective organization to achieve membership in the Afghanistan Chamber of Commerce & Industry, has become a memorable monument and a source of hope for every woman trader and businesswoman in this land. During this time, with the positive support of the majority, we actively participated as energetic members of the Board of the Afghanistan Chamber of Commerce & Industry, along with our colleagues, paving innovative and effective pathways for women's presence in decision-making positions.

The key to transformation

Any program implemented within a society that lays the foundation for major transformations should not be overlooked. These programs have the potential to create profound and lasting impacts on social structures and processes, gradually becoming milestones in history.

Carefully and transparently designed programs that accurately consider social needs and wills can connect individuals and strengthen a sense of community and belonging. By fostering such connections, these programs can contribute to the growth and advancement of societies and cultures, ultimately becoming essential parts of a nation's history.

In designing these programs, attention must be paid to social, economic, cultural, and political aspects. Additionally, participation and transparency in the decision-making process are of paramount importance. Individuals must feel that their opinions and needs are genuinely valued, and their involvement in decision-making is respected.

Predicting the future impacts of a program and determining optimal pathways to achieve common goals are also vital aspects. Commitment to ethical principles and long-term objectives, rather than short-term decisions, enables these programs to effect positive changes in communities.

Ultimately, any program adhering to these principles can be a significant step toward improving social structure and public life. Therefore, valuing these programs and maintaining continuous oversight of their implementation is key to ensuring their lasting impact and historical significance.

Milestones in women's commercial development

Over the past three decades, the history of women's trade in Afghanistan has witnessed remarkable transformations. These changes have not only strengthened women's economic position in society but have also paved the way for a dynamic commercial and economic landscape. These shifts have marked significant milestones in women's economic development and have played a crucial role in their empowerment.

In the early years, the establishment of the Khorasan Trade Cooperative, was a bold initiative that facilitated women's entry into the world of commerce. This cooperative, formed with the goal of women's economic empowerment, was the first step toward financial independence and the development of women's entrepreneurial capacities.

Two years later, in 1995, the Habitat Women's Community Forums played a key role in providing various services for women. These organizations created social and economic infrastructures that enabled women to expand their business activities and gain a more significant share in local and national markets. These initial efforts not only boosted women's confidence in their capabilities but also laid the groundwork for the establishment of stronger trade institutions in the future.

With the turn of the century, the year 2003 marked another significant milestone with the establishment of the Afghanistan Women's Business Council. As the first official institution, this council provided a structured platform for coordinating, developing, and supporting women's business activities. In addition to offering educational and advisory services, the council connected women entrepreneurs with domestic and international business networks, playing a pivotal role in shaping their independent commercial identity.

Building on this progress, the year 2007 saw the establishment of the Afghan Women's Business Federation. Formed to strengthen women's business networks, this federation became a comprehensive institution for supporting women entrepreneurs. Key activities such as training programs, investment opportunities, and strengthening international relations helped solidify women's position in the country's economic landscape.

In 2017, a crucial and transformative step was taken in women's trade. The founding of the Afghanistan Women's Chamber of Commerce & Industry marked a new phase of progress, organization, and empowerment in this field. This institution not only served as a support centre but also enabled women to engage in diverse sectors of trade, industry, and investment. Through development programs, training workshops, and financial and technical support, the chamber significantly impacted women's economic growth.

The journey travelled so far is a proud and influential narrative of Afghan women's role in commerce. These institutions and organizations have flourished like colourful flowers in Afghanistan's business landscape, making substantial contributions to the prosperity of the sector. These advancements not only highlight Afghan women's immense economic potential but also promise a bright and hopeful future for them.

Although the path to development has always been accompanied by challenges such as legal restrictions, cultural barriers, and economic crises, past experiences have demonstrated that Afghan women, with perseverance, creativity, and unique abilities, can overcome these obstacles. Despite all difficulties, the future of women's trade in Afghanistan remains on a trajectory of growth, sustainability, and innovation, opening new horizons for women entrepreneurs and professionals in this fundamentally important field.

Chapter 14
Trade in the shadow of limitations

Determination and progress despite restrictions

The reopening of the Afghanistan Women's Chamber of Commerce & Industry after the fall of the Republic and the return of the Taliban on August 15, 2021, was not only a significant event but also a historic moment that reflected the will, courage, and power of Afghan women. In days when the country was grappling with chaos and political changes, and under circumstances where women faced numerous restrictions, this act symbolized the steadfastness and relentless efforts of Afghan women in their pursuit of freedom and rights.

With the imposition of severe restrictions and bans, especially on women's economic activities, the social and economic fabric of Afghanistan underwent profound changes. However, in these very circumstances, Afghan women, with determination and resolve, decided to embark on a new path and continue to play their roles in the economic and social spheres. They feared nothing and, through persistent efforts, managed to secure permission for the reopening of the Afghanistan Women's Chamber of Commerce & Industry despite the harsh and challenging conditions.

After an eight-month hiatus and despite political and social pressures, the Chamber was able to resume its activities in Kabul and other parts of the country. Although the situation for women entrepreneurs under these restrictions is complicated, their resilience in these difficult circumstances showcases the hidden strength within the will of Afghan women.

According to reports from the Afghanistan Women's Chamber of Commerce & Industry, approximately 800 women are active in various sectors. Some of these women are the sole breadwinners of their families, and their livelihood is primarily sustained through small-scale businesses. These women bear significant responsibilities and challenges, and they can stand firm against the toughest of conditions.

Afghan women are courageously engaged in various economic and social sectors. They are recognized not only as providers for their families but also as symbols of powerful and creative women in Afghanistan. Despite the challenges they face, these women contribute to the cultural and social advancement of their country. They represent a new beginning for the growth of women's economy in Afghanistan, akin to narcissus flowers blooming in winter, continuing to inspire life and hope.

This story is not only about Afghan women; it is a narrative of contemporary Afghan history, reflecting a nation's struggle for social, cultural, and economic justice. Women who have kept the flag of determination and courage high in these conditions are truly the pioneers of a monumental transformation in the history of their country.

Through their economic activities, Afghan women are not only contributing to the growth and development of the country but also playing an important role in achieving cultural and social goals. They are at the heart of families, communities, and the nation, building a better and more prosperous future for themselves and future generations. These women are recognized as sources of inspiration for all those seeking progress and the betterment of their communities.

What sets these women apart is their unparalleled determination and firm belief in their abilities. Amid challenges, crises, and threats, they remain steadfast, overcoming limitations. With every step they take towards progress, they demonstrate that nothing can stand in the way of their iron will.

In this context, there is an increasing need for research and documentation of the activities of Afghan women. A thorough investigation of the fundamental factors and reasons that have led to the successes of these women in the face of adversity is essential for future foresight and to benefit from their experiences. Accurately documenting these stories and realities will not only preserve history but also serve as a model for future generations.

Afghan women must tell their own history to ensure that these stories are correctly recorded and introduced to the world. In this process, every narrative, every experience, and every step these women have taken must be carefully documented so that everyone can benefit from these invaluable lessons.

Ultimately, Afghan women, with every step they take, are shaping the history of their country. And this story is just the beginning of a tale that will continue – a story of Afghan women who, with courage and hope, move toward a brighter future in the heart of every crisis.

Reflections on the role of women entrepreneurs in history

Women entrepreneurs have always played a significant and historical role in society. From educational programs in Afghanistan's school system, which included sewing, tailoring, and home management, to the establishment of the Women's Institute in 1943, proposed by Zainab Dawood, these initiatives have paved the way for women's empowerment. This institute included a kindergarten, school, cinema, and other facilities, where adult women and mothers learned to read and write while selling their handicrafts to earn an income.

The establishment of the first women's cooperative for sewing and weaving in the mid-1990s and the creation of Women's Community Forums in 1995 further highlight the contributions of these women. The founding of the Afghanistan Women's Business Council, later the Afghanistan Women's Business Federation, and the emergence of the Afghanistan Women's Chamber of Commerce & Industry, reflect the extensive impact of women in entrepreneurship and trade.

These women, with determination and strong motivation, have been able to overcome traditional and cultural barriers to play active roles in various economic sectors. During times of war and economic crises, many women supported their families by starting small businesses and were even recognized as successful managers of large enterprises.

A notable success story is that of Suraya Faizi. Her handcrafted works – including crocheting, children's clothing, and decorative fabrics – gained widespread recognition. She not only achieved self-sufficiency but also created job opportunities for others Over time, her workshop grew into a reputable company, with its products reaching international markets.

Afghan women entrepreneurs have achieved remarkable progress not only in traditional areas such as handicrafts, but also in modern fields like technology and e-commerce. There are numerous success stories – for example, the creation of online platforms that allow members of various women's business associations to sell handmade products, resulting in substantial income. It is important to compile a list of these entrepreneurs and highlight their stories, so they can inspire other women to pursue opportunities in business.

Women's markets in Kabul: a place for hope and rebuilding lives

In the heart of bustling Kabul, two special gardens tell the story of Afghan women's resilience and determination: Shahrara Women's Garden and Babur Garden. These spaces are more than marketplaces – they are sanctuaries for art, solidarity, and self-empowerment.

In Shahrara Garden, rebuilt in 2008 (1387), a market with around 30 shops was established to offer women entrepreneurs a peaceful and safe space to sell their products freely. It's a place for conversation, learning, and belonging – where women are not just vendors, but the true owners of the space. But Shahrara Garden, once a haven of hope and self-empowerment for women, now remains closed under the shadow of restrictions.

In Babur Garden, with its royal history and majestic setting, women showcase their handmade crafts in 14 permanent shops and weekly markets held in a beautifully restored caravanserai. The sound of sewing machines, the colours of embroidery, and the aroma of fresh tea bring life to the stone walls and historic ambiance.

In this market, some women have not only built their own businesses, but also founded a union that supports dozens of others. Every day, they open their shops with hope, arranging their own products and those of their members – waiting for a customer, maybe a local or foreign visitor, whose small purchase could help sustain a household. These shops in Babur Garden are more than commercial spaces, they represent steady rebuilding, and a vision for a brighter future for the women of Afghanistan.

These achievements demonstrate that with appropriate support and encouragement, women can play a crucial role in the economic and social development of the country. Thus, focusing on the education and empowerment of women, creating conducive conditions for entrepreneurship, and supporting women-owned businesses are of paramount importance. This approach not only improves the economic status of women but also leads to sustainable and balanced national development.

Pioneering women even under the restrictions imposed by the Taliban illustrate how they continue to innovate and contribute to the community. These actions represent a quiet revolution, showcasing resilience and determination in impossibly challenging circumstances.

One woman's story of resilience and empowerment from Kabul to Bamyan

Laila Arab Shahi is a name that truly embodies the spirit of resilience. She is one of the most prominent and dynamic figures in social and economic spheres. Born in Kabul and belonging to the Hazara ethnic group, Laila joined the ranks of committed women entrepreneurs in 2005, determined from the outset to learn and teach.

For many years, she worked in various administrative roles within the Federation – as a capable trainer, she participated in numerous programs with the Afghanistan Women's Business Council. Her notable presence and activities in the council, especially in social development projects like *Through the Garden Gate*, played a crucial role in educating and raising awareness among rural women from 2007 to 2011. During these years, she established a union that created work and training opportunities for many women.

However, with the Taliban's takeover of Afghanistan and the imposition of severe restrictions on women's activities, Laila was not spared from this relentless wave. Her activities were halted or suspended, leading her to migrate to Bamyan city. Now, she lives in Bamyan with her family, including her two children and husband. Despite the challenging circumstances, Laila has maintained her spirit and has reached out to assist the people of Bamyan. She has created work opportunities not only for women but also for men in the agriculture sector.

Utilizing the techniques she employed in the *Through the Garden Gate* program, Leila is active among women in the villages of Bamyan. This is a quiet revolution – an effort to maintain balance in the current conditions while striving for a better future for the community and the country.

These achievements demonstrate that with appropriate support and encouragement, women can continue to play a significant role in the economic and social development of the nation. Therefore, focusing on the education and empowerment of women, creating conducive conditions for entrepreneurship, and supporting women-owned businesses is of utmost importance. This not only improves the economic status of women but also leads to sustainable and balanced development for the country.

Laila is engaged in educating women in Bamyan and with enthusiasm, she asks, "What should we do so that we women can shape our own future socially and economically?" She encourages women to believe in their abilities and to pursue learning new skills. By organizing workshops in various fields such as agriculture, handicrafts, and entrepreneurship, Laila strives to provide them with the tools necessary to create and manage their own businesses.

She emphasizes the importance of collaboration and solidarity among women, stating, "If we work together and share our experiences, we can create real and lasting changes." With this question, Laila inspires women who are striving to shape their own destinies and build a brighter future for themselves and their families.

The results of Laila's efforts – a group of women can be seen alongside the men in their families, preparing to improve their agricultural activities using the tools and equipment provided.

Her goal is to provide diverse training to farmers and artisans using personal and volunteer experiences. These trainings focus on sustainable development, self-sufficiency, and the revitalization of local resources, designed to create new economic and job opportunities for women while preserving the authenticity and cultural heritage of the region. The aim, through this approach, is to not only empower women and future generations but also to create pathways for improving the lives of those who have been economically and socially marginalized.

Laila is also engaging in discussions with local men, including intellectuals and community leaders, about the basic challenges and needs of both women and men in various neighbourhoods. She is seeking ways to address these issues and strengthen mutual support on social and economic matters by collaborating with different groups.

She has also established the *Bamyan Farm School* where women farmers gather periodically or as needed on their own farms to discuss and exchange ideas about their strengths and weaknesses. Laila, who has learned agricultural techniques through the programs and the Afghanistan Women's Business Council, shares her experiences with these women farmers. In this way, these experiences are shared during practical gatherings on the farm, enabling the production of higher-quality products and increasing their income.

A *Celebration of Teacher's Day* is an opportunity to honour and celebrate the invaluable role of teachers in educating and shaping generations. This day is dedicated to recognizing the tireless efforts and contributions of teachers towards nurturing minds and guiding students forwards to a brighter future. On this day, students and communities hold special events, present gifts, and express their gratitude to teachers. Teachers, as the backbone of every society, not only impart academic knowledge and skills but also play a crucial role in the moral and social development of individuals, on society and sustainable development.

A day with mild weather begins in Bamyan. The cool morning breeze gently rustles the leaves of the trees, and the sun slowly rises from behind the towering mountains. On this pleasant morning, a group of Bamyan teachers have gathered in a simple, old house, away from prying eyes, to celebrate *Teacher's Day*.

This house, with its plastered ceiling and whitewashed mud walls, is a relic of bygone years, holding untold stories within its walls. The room where the teachers have gathered is a silent witness to the fact that for the past three years, the Taliban have taken control of the country, restricting the presence of women in schools and public life. It has been three years since Bamyan girls have been deprived of their right to education beyond the sixth grade. The sound of girls' laughter and joy in schoolyards is absent, replaced by a deep silence and sorrow. Yet, amidst this darkness, flames of hope continue to burn.

The female teachers of Bamyan, attending this gathering, have decided to keep hope alive despite all the obstacles and dangers they face. They are well aware of the great risk involved in gathering at this house, but their hearts beat with hope and a deep longing for the return of girls to schools and freedom for all the women of Afghanistan.

Laila, one of the seasoned teachers of Bamyan, who has devoted her entire life to educating girls, glances around the room. She closes her eyes, remembering the days when little girls would eagerly come to her classes, filled with endless questions and dreams that soared to the sky. A bittersweet smile forms on her lips. Now, in this small house, she and the other women teachers are trying to revive those dreams.

Each teacher in the room has a story to tell. Sara, who once taught mathematics, speaks through tears about the last day she saw her students in the classroom. They looked to the future with hope and enthusiasm, but now...

Maryam, who taught Persian literature, speaks about the power of words and the poetry of Rumi and Hafez. She believes that words can bring change, that they can empower and keep hope alive. In this gathering, she recites poems that warm the hearts and spirits of everyone present.

Simin, who organized this gathering, speaks with a firm and hopeful voice: "We are here to show the world that we are still alive, that we still have hope, and that we can still give hope to others. We are teachers; we are the builders of the future, and no one can take that from us."

Despite the risks that threaten them, these women have decided to stand firm. At this meeting, they make plans for the secret education of girls, strategies to deliver books and educational resources to them, and ways to maintain morale and hope in their community. As the gathering concludes, the women leave the house one by one. They know the road ahead is difficult, but they have faith that they can make a difference. As they step outside, a soft, gentle light from the sun touches their faces. This light symbolizes the hope alive in their hearts, the hope that one day the girls of

Bamyan will once again sit in classrooms, with smiles full of hope and a bright future ahead.

This is the story of women who stand in darkness and draw the light toward themselves, the story of teachers who, with love and sacrifice, dream of a better future for the girls and women of Bamyan and all of Afghanistan.

Laila, a woman with remarkable strength and determination, stands bravely and spares no effort in serving her community. Through consultations with local councils, she developed a bold plan to provide 24 hand-operated mini-tractors to farmers in the Shibertu, Qarghanatu, and Shaheedan councils in the heart of Bamyan. Every meeting and every session were an opportunity for her to prove that a woman, too, could pave the way for change and progress.

On the morning of Wednesday, April 17, 2024, as the sun rose, the Women's Social and Economic Services Institute, led by Laila Arab Shahi, proudly took centre stage. A lively ceremony was held, where the governor of Bamyan, the head of agriculture, irrigation, and livestock, along with other local officials and families of farmers – both men and women – witnessed a major technological achievement. The distribution of modern tractors was a symbol of hope and progress for the farmers, who would now be able to prepare their lands and expand their agricultural production with this new technology.

In a time when heavy restrictions have been placed on women, Laila, with wisdom and courage, carved her own path to engage with authorities and, by providing necessary facilities, won the trust and approval of the people. She proved that women can not only have a presence in society but also play a vital and influential role.

The governor of Bamyan, with admiration and respect, urged the farmers and local councils to unite and make the most of these tractors, paving the way for a brighter future for themselves and future generations. With every step she takes, Laila continues to highlight and elevate the role of women in society. She stands as a symbol of strength, hope, and transformation.

Laila continues to proudly celebrate *International Day of the Girl*. From a young age, she shapes her daughter's character and teaches her to take pride in all her identities. Laila chooses a traditional outfit for her daughter; however, this outfit represents more than just one ethnic group. The attire and style of Laila's daughter reflect all the nationalities of this land. In her dress, signs of Hazara, Pashtun, Turkmen, Uzbek, Tajik, Pashahee, and Nuristani cultures can be seen.

Through this simple yet profound act, Laila conveys a message of solidarity and unity. She wants her daughter to learn from an early age that the value of individuals lies in their diverse identities, not in their differences. Every time she looks at her daughter, she is reminded that these girls are the future builders of society and must grow up in an environment filled with love and respect for all ethnicities and cultures. With every step she takes, Laila wishes for a better world, free from prejudice, for her daughter and all the girls of her homeland.

Yet, despite all these hopes, Laila's heart is filled with concern; what will her daughter's future be like under the restrictions imposed by the Taliban? With all her being, she wants her daughter to receive education beyond the sixth grade, to continue to the twelfth grade, to attend university, and ultimately to serve her community and people. Will these dreams come true under such prohibitions? This is a question Laila reflects on every day, but her hope and faith in the future remain resolutely strong.

Chapter 15
A new story of the heart

Migrating to London

In the early hours of a fluttering year in 2012, my heart was heavy with the pain of separation from the beauty of life in my homeland. The airplane, like a foreign vessel, carried me to the unknown shores of London. The only thing I had with me was my love for life, packed tightly in a suitcase.

At that moment, when I couldn't say goodbye to my relatives, friends, and colleagues, I was overwhelmed with sadness. They remained in Afghanistan, while I drifted away from familiar scenes and memories. This distance weighed heavily on my heart, filled with beautiful memories that accompanied me with every step.

Traveling to London was a new and unknown experience for me. My suitcase held not only personal belongings but also fresh hopes and innovative dreams. This city was ready with a range of emotions and new challenges for us. Yet, at every moment, memories of Afghanistan's green fields and the kind faces of my friends were with me.

In my thoughts, scenes of farewell with family, the colourful flowers of Afghanistan, and moments of peace with friends were etched. These visions, like beautiful paintings, stirred my mind and filled my heart with deep emotions. With a heart full of longing for my homeland, I realized that a part of me would always remain in Afghanistan. Yet, with each step I took, I tried to keep that love and will to live close, motivating me to create a new life in this distant land.

Upon my arrival in this vibrant city, adorned with colourful flags, the roads were bustling, and the sounds of urban life filled the air. Countless faces from various backgrounds moved around me, and everything felt fresh – from the language to the scents and tastes of life. As I walked the lively streets of London, a mix of longing and loneliness accompanied my steps. This vast city introduced itself as one of the distant lands of immigrant life. In every glance and moment, new wonders awaited me. Yet, my heart still trembled for the unique beauty hidden behind my mind's veil.

Every corner of this city told stories in different languages. The myriad experiences of immigrants intertwined in this bustling metropolis in countless ways. Yet deep within me, a constant feeling emerged – a sense that with the passage of time, I was no longer alone. Each day, I felt renewed hope and enthusiasm rising within me. London, in fact, soon became a home – once daunting and unfamiliar, it had now turned into my closest friend. This experience showed that the love for our memories and past stories can bind us to the land we left behind and help us rediscover ourselves.

The first year of my life in London was filled with challenges and hardships. I was seeking work and language education while connecting with Afghan women, both in London and through outreach efforts to inspire those back in Afghanistan. In this way, I shared my experiences and sought solutions to their problems. I dedicated myself to volunteer opportunities in my community, providing services wherever I could. I shared my experiences with those women, seeking solutions to their difficulties. I wholeheartedly dedicated myself to every volunteer opportunity in my neighbourhood with various local organizations. From the very beginning, my passion and enthusiasm drove me to seek work opportunities and learn the language. Throughout this time, I connected with various people in the community, and through continuous effort and high determination, I was able to improve my English skills.

Another significant aspect of my life in London was my connection to my sons, daughter-in-law, and grandchildren. The oldest was just four years old when I arrived. Supporting and caring for them brought me immense joy, and my support helped Zala, Saba, and Sara grow. Their mother completed her professional education and worked at a reputable company in London.

In dark and sorrowful moments, I often reflected on my pain and longing. Yet, I held onto the hope of seeing my own dear mother again someday. I would talk to her on the phone, and I could hear her lively voice. Each time, she would eagerly say, "Come see me, come calm my heart." The hardships and obstacles that blocked my way to see my family intensified my longing. Legal and security issues stood like an insurmountable wall between me and my mother and older sister. Each time I sought a way to overcome these barriers, my heart ached, and I lamented deeply.

After migrating from Iran, my dear mother spent her life receiving treatment for various ailments she faced over the years. Following a complicated surgery due to a broken foot, her life became fraught with challenges. Yet, with the strength and determination within her, she always tried to resist difficulties. After the operation and treatment, my mother's heart could no longer endure, and she left this world shortly thereafter. The loss of my beloved ones left a profound wound in my heart, but the memories of my mother's life remain etched in my mind.

Every time I spoke with her on the phone, I could hear the weary breath of her past struggles, especially when recalling my father's early death and my mother's efforts to keep our family together during hard times. This story was filled with challenges, yet their strong resolve allowed them to continue living. The loss of my father, mother, and my older sister Rabia filled my heart with sorrow. Yet, their memories and life experiences continuously guided me along a path of hope and resilience. This life story was full of bright visions and longings I learned to live with daily.

Spring journeys

Every year, just as the spring flowers begin to bloom in our hearts, we set off once again on a heartfelt journey to visit our beloved daughter and dear grandchildren in Sweden. These trips are always filled with moments of joy and tranquillity – moments spent with loved ones who, in a land far from our own, keep the light of love and determination shining brightly for us.

My daughter, Nilab, and my grandchildren – Lima, Elaha, Marwa, and Elham – welcome us each year with warm hospitality. They are always eager and full of excitement, awaiting our arrival with open arms and joyful hearts.

Each time we travel to Sweden, the fresh air flowing through the train windows fills our hearts with a sense of renewal, reminding us that we are on our way to see our loved ones. Everywhere we look, greenery and blooming flowers seem to greet us, gently guiding us toward the cozy home of our daughter.

Whenever we step into the house, the smiling faces of my grandchildren fill our hearts with a unique kind of joy and freshness. Every moment of these visits becomes a cherished memory.

At night, my grandchildren gather around me with enthusiasm. Their eagerness to hear stories from the past builds a bridge between yesterday and today. Each one listens intently and warmly, and through my storytelling, I share with them the bittersweet moments of my life, passing on my experiences to their young hearts.

On these nights, time transforms into an endless circle of tales and memories. As time goes by, each grandchild carefully and respectfully turns our experiences into part of our family's legacy. These stories strengthen our bond with the past and help them realize just how precious they truly are.

At the end of each journey, we return home with hearts full of laughter and sweet memories. These trips remind us that the bond with family is always life's most meaningful and beautiful journey.

A brief journey homeward – reconnecting roots

In August 2023, as the plane touched down in Afghanistan, a wave of emotions washed over me. I had returned to my homeland after years of longing, and the feeling was indescribable. This journey wasn't just about reuniting with family and friends; it was a spiritual pilgrimage to reconnect with my roots, culture, and identity.

The moment I stepped outside the airport, the warm, dusty air of Kabul enveloped me. The familiar scent brought a rush of nostalgia and belonging. Despite the ongoing challenges Afghanistan faced, the resilience of its people shone through their welcoming smiles and outstretched hands. It was a clear reminder that home isn't just a place; it's the people who make it special.

My first stop was my childhood home. As I stepped into the yard, memories flooded back – laughter from my siblings, the aroma of my mother's cooking, and the calming presence of my father. Though the house had suffered from time and conflict, its walls still echoed the stories of my past. The absence of my parents hung heavily in the air, a painful reminder of the losses my family had endured during years of turmoil.

Next, I visited the local market, a vibrant hub of activity filled with the bright colours of traditional Afghan clothing and the scent of freshly baked bread. This small market was a living testament to the resilience of the Afghan people. Shopkeepers greeted me warmly, and I felt a sense of unity and camaraderie that transcended the hardships they faced daily.

Reuniting with friends was one of the highlights of my journey. We had all scattered across the globe during years of conflict, each of us in search of safety and a better life. Now, sitting together, we shared stories of our journeys and hopes for Afghanistan's future. Our shared laughter and tears reflected the deep bonds forged through years of struggle.

One of the sweetest moments of my trip was meeting my nieces, nephews, and the children of my cousin for the first time. Those who had been born in my absence or had grown into young adults symbolized hope and new beginnings. As I embraced them, I couldn't help but think of the countless Afghan children who deserve a future filled with peace, education, and opportunity.

A story of sisters and a flicker of hope

During my month in Kabul in August 2023, I had the opportunity to visit Selma and Diana, two sisters who were once vibrant students at Kabul University. However, the challenging circumstances they faced transformed that vibrancy into something bittersweet. Their smiles, once full of hope and promise, now seemed muted, lacking the brightness of a hopeful future. The sparkle that had once filled their eyes was replaced with a heaviness that spoke volumes about their struggles. Meeting them left a profound impression on me, a stark reminder of the dreams that remain unfulfilled for so many.

In the quiet of the room, Selma spoke softly, her words forever etched in my memory as one of the most painful moments. She recounted her days of studying passionately at university, filled with big dreams. Yet, after two years of interrupted education, all those aspirations had vanished amidst the dust of restrictions. With sadness, she said, "I spend each day in this house without any purpose. The days of thinking about a bright future feel long gone. I feel like a prisoner in a meaningless life."

She spoke of the depression and anxiety that had cast shadows over her during this time. Thoughts of an uncertain future robbed her of sleep at night. With a choked voice, she expressed, "My only wish is to return to university and achieve the dreams I once had. But each day, I feel further away from them."

Sitting in that house, listening to Selma, painted a grim picture of a generation whose dreams were trapped behind walls of limitation. Selma, once a girl who looked forward to the future, now waited within the confines of her home for days that might never come.

Selma was once a girl with eyes full of dreams, who planted seeds of hope and motivation with every step she took through the bustling streets of Kabul. A second-year geology student at Kabul University, she was passionate about learning and research, her heart filled with aspirations as sturdy as Afghanistan's towering mountains. Every day, she would tell herself, "I can do this; I will reach my goals one day."

But then the situation began to change as the Taliban returned to power. Universities were closed, and the doors to knowledge were locked for Selma and thousands of other girls. Where she had once looked towards a bright future, she was now confined within the walls of her home. Her silent screams ascended to the sky, cries that only her own heart could hear.

Initially, Selma remained hopeful. She would say to herself, "This too shall pass. I will return to university and pursue my dreams." But days turned into weeks, and weeks into months, with Selma still sitting aimlessly in a corner of her house.

The days once filled with big dreams had turned into nightmares that woke her in the night. Restrictions were like invisible chains, binding her hands and erasing her dreams one by one. Once seeking the unknown in the expansive mountains and valleys of Afghanistan, she was now imprisoned by her thoughts in a small room.

Every day, Selma gazed out of the small window of her home at the sky and asked herself, "Is there a future for me? Will I ever return to my university classes?" Yet, the more she pondered, the deeper she sank into a sea of stress and depression. The thought of an uncertain and despair-filled future engulfed her.

Despite the heartbreak, a small flame of hope still flickered in her heart. Selma continued to cling to the hope of returning to university, flipping through her geology books, and breaking free from the chains of limitations. She yearned for the day she could reach her dreams, shining like distant stars in the sky.

Selma understood that the path ahead was difficult and dark, but she whispered to herself, "Nothing lasts forever. One day, I will rise again." Perhaps it was this small flame that saved her from falling into irrecoverable depths of despair. She knew that her dreams might have turned into sleep, but no sleep is everlasting.

In the end, my month-long trip to Afghanistan was a profound reminder of the unbreakable bonds that tie us to our roots. The feeling of returning as an Afghan woman after eleven years was a complex mix of joy, sorrow, hope, and determination. It stands as a testament to the enduring spirit of a people facing unimaginable challenges, still striving for a brighter future for themselves and their country.

Forging a new cultural unity

My life in London has become a rich and enlightening journey. This path is filled with new opportunities and unique experiences, each teaching me a valuable lesson. As I explore the historical and cultural corners of this city and engage in diverse activities, I continuously learn and grow.

In addition to my personal growth, I actively support businesswomen striving for progress and promptly provide humanitarian aid to those in need in Afghanistan. For nearly two years, I have also volunteered at the Beacontree Children's Centre in Barking and Dagenham, which has profoundly impacted my perspective and understanding.

In London, I maintain friendly and lasting relationships with friends, peers, fellow countrymen, and relatives, leveraging our shared experiences across various fields. I am grateful to have built a community of friends from diverse races, ethnicities, and nationalities. Despite our cultural and linguistic differences, we are united by mutual respect and empathy. This unity allows us to benefit from friendly gatherings, share our experiences and ideas, and collaborate for guidance whenever needed. Every moment of this journey reminds me of my homeland and highlights the longing for similar opportunities back home. While Afghan women face limitations in education and work, these experiences inspire my hope for a brighter future.

Final thoughts

This book is not only a testament to my remarkable life but also a mirror reflecting how determination, love, and resilience can bring about positive change in society. May it serve as inspiration for all who read it. I hope it will encourage individuals, families, and communities, by looking to the past, draw from their experiences and, while always honouring local values, move toward a brighter and more hopeful future.

At the heart of this narrative lies a powerful reminder that in respecting our history and local values, we can shape our shared future. This tale underscores that every small step we take can lead to broader progress and transformation. Together, we can create a world filled with hope and humanity.

A rich and diverse collection of credible sources were used in the process of compiling and writing this work. These sources, which include specialized articles, reputable books, various interviews, and in-depth and credible reports, provide extensive information about the history, politics, and socio-cultural context of Afghanistan. Among them, some sources focus on historical analyses, while others are based on direct observations and interviews with prominent figures and social activists.

However, many of the events and stories narrated in this book are based on my own personal experiences and observations regarding the historical and economic developments in Afghanistan, the history of women's trade, and social efforts to promote women's rights. These experiences, which are presented in a detailed and documented manner, offer a real and profound view of the status of women in Afghanistan, particularly as they have influenced my own life. These memoirs, with accuracy and honesty, present a unique and authentic picture of the challenges, resistances, and achievements of Afghan women.

This combination of sources and personal accounts have been included in order to create a fully documented and realistic portrayal of the situation of women in Afghanistan so that everyone can become more deeply and accurately acquainted with the issues and challenges of women in this country.

In a constantly changing world, women's progress and empowerment are not just a moral duty, but a social and economic necessity. Social and economic development programs have the power to improve the fate of women and empower them in various fields. We need to ensure that the needs and rights of half the population are not overlooked in any program or reform and understand that the role of women in advancing societies and achieving sustainable goals is paramount. The position of women, with their capabilities and talents, plays a vital role in achieving balance and progress. Such recognition can only encourage equal opportunities and respect for human rights. Empowering the roles and active participation of women in every field of life is proven to generate enormous improvements in communities and contributes positively to the advancement and development of society.

As you close this book, I invite you to view these stories as motivation to embark on a new phase in your own life. Trust in your power, respect one another, and recognize that each of us can add meaning and colour to our lives while contributing value to the world around us. Let us courageously share stories of change, hope, and impact, building a world where everyone believes in their ideals.

www.ingramcontent.com/pod-product-compliance
Lightning Source LLC
Chambersburg PA
CBHW051257020426
42333CB00026B/3245